IN A STRANGE LAND
Short Stories for Creative Learning

Originality is the essence of true scholarship.
Creativity is the soul of the true scholar.

                                              Nnamdi Azikiwe

IN A STRANGE LAND
Short Stories for Creative Learning

Andrzej Cirocki
Alicia Peña Calvo

IN A STRANGE LAND

Short Stories for Creative Learning

Andrzej Cirocki and Alicia Peña Calvo have asserted their right under the Copyright, Designs and Patents Act, 1988 to be identified as the authors of this work.

Proofreading: Michael Butler, Marie-Christin Strobel
Editorial consultant: Ann Claypole

ISBN: 9783734789465

First edition

Copyright © 2015 LinguaBooks

www.linguabooks.com

Every effort has been made to trace the holders of intellectual property rights and the publishers will be happy to correct any mistakes or omissions in future editions.

All rights reserved. No part of this publication may be reproduced, stored in a retrieval system or transmitted, in any form or by any means, electronic, mechanical, photocopying, recording or otherwise, without the prior permission of the publishers.

Herstellung und Verlag: BoD - Books on Demand, Norderstedt
Printed in Germany

Bibliografische Information der Deutschen Bibliothek:

Die Deutsche Bibliothek verzeichnet diese Publikation in der Deutschen Nationalbibliografie; detaillierte bibliografische Daten sind im Internet über <http://dnb.ddb.de> abrufbar.

This book is sold subject to the condition that it shall not, by way of trade or otherwise, be lent, re-sold, hired out or otherwise circulated without the publisher's prior consent in any form of binding or cover other than that in which it is published and without a similar condition including this condition being imposed on the subsequent purchaser.

Layout and design: Maurice Claypole

Contents

Acknowledgements 7
To the Teacher 8
To the Learner 10

THE BLUE DRAGON 11
Outline of activities 12
Story 13
Activities:
1 **Pre-reading:** Talking about emotions 28
2 **Visualising and predicting:** Focusing on the title and the opening ... 29
3 **Empathising:** Understanding the language of feelings 30
4 **Creative writing:** Inventing a fictional character 31
5 **Extension and experimentation:** Making videos 32

THROUGH WALLS 33
Outline of activities 34
Story 35
Activities:
1 **Pre-reading:** Talking about meaning, effect and context 48
2 **Engaging with the text:** Analysing and discussing specific aspects ... 51
3 **Exploring the story:** Making connections 53
4 **Extension and experimentation:** Sequencing events and
   developing the story 56

DON'T GO IN 59

Outline of activities.. 60

Story.. 61

Activities:

1   **Pre-reading:** Discussing first impressions 76
2   **Expressing emotions:** Understanding and using similes 77
3   **Thinking beyond the text:** Interpreting dreams................................ 79
4   **Improvisation:** Reporting problems on the phone 81
5   **Experimentation:** Making a television programme and
    writing a letter 82
6   **Extension:** Designing a movie poster 84

MERLIN 85

Outline of activities.. 86

Story.. 87

Activities:

1   **Pre-reading:** Predicting the story line 100
2   **Listening and writing:** Forming and describing first impressions ... 103
3   **Expressing feelings and opinions:** Posting comments on a blog 104
4   **Improvisation:** Acting out a court-room drama 105
5   **Creative writing:** Producing a haiku 106
6   **Extension:** Discussing opinions found on an internet forum.......... 107

Acknowledgements

We wish to sincerely thank Susan M. Dean, Hannah C. Floyd, Lynn A. Fraser and Tracey Seagrove for writing these stories for us and allowing us to include them in this collection. Special thanks go to Alison Bruce, Royal Literary Fund Fellow from Anglia Ruskin University, who helped us to select the stories for this volume. Next, we would like to extend our thanks and gratitude to Paul Bloomfield, Michael Butler, Lorraine Noble and Mary Whiteside, who kindly agreed to read the stories for the accompanying audio material, and to Will Smythe for preparing the recording.

The accompanying audio recordings are available as two audio CDs or as individual MP3 downloads. For more information, please see the publisher's website at www.linguabooks.com.

To the Teacher

IN A STRANGE LAND is a collection of four stories written with the aim of providing you with motivating and engaging material to use in the classroom at the CEFR B2 and C1 levels. The stories require the reader to represent the imaginative world while they interact with the texts. Encouraging the reader to become an active participant in the story not only offers fertile ground for critical thinking, but also helps the student to develop scope for mental reflection on the texts they read, as well as on how the plot relates to their personal life.

These original stories invite the student to read naturally in a relaxed and enjoyable manner. For this reason, it is not our intention to encourage you to exploit these stories in the conventional form of intensive reading we find in many modern course books. Since the stories have been written to be enjoyed, they are supported with attractive activities in which the student can integrate all language skills, use computer technology, practise learning strategies and exercise autonomy. In other words, the student is involved in experiential learning through which they are stimulated to relate the inner world of their own selves to the outer world of external reality.

In order to arrive at a compromise between a truly natural reading experience and what the language teacher and learner often expect from texts, we would suggest two ways of using this material: reading for pleasure and an integrated skills approach to reading.

The reading for pleasure approach is based on Pennac's *Rights of the Reader*. We offer the following two alternatives to the learner: to read the story and enjoy it, both in and out of the classroom, or to read the story while listening to a recording of it (audio-reading).

The integrated skills approach combines both receptive and productive skills in activities based on specific aspects of the stories in this volume. The learner is involved in a series of creative activities which encourage meaningful use of the target language. The skills practised and the types of activities vary from story to story. By the time the learner gets to the final activity in each story, they will have practised the language related to its content, including relevant vocabulary. Occasionally, the skills practice is supported by vocabulary exploitation exercises to help the language learner to interact with the text.

It is our intention to promote a creative and original approach to reading. We believe that the input required to stimulate effective language acquisition and learning should engage the whole person. For this reason, the stories and activities in this volume aim to boost learner-intrinsic motivation, affective arousal and self-investment. Additionally, this material instantly attracts the learner's curiosity, interest and attention, all of which are necessary for successful language development. Another distinctive feature of this volume is that reading encourages the language learner to use the target language in a new and productive manner.

The activities are ready to use, yet you are welcome to adapt them to meet your students' needs and interests. It is essential for teachers to exercise their creativity, to recognise the need for contextual relevance and to address the learning styles of both individuals and members of a reading community. This differentiated approach maximises the potential of each language learner to extend their learning. Matching classroom work to the diverse abilities of the learners requires teachers to abandon the security of the structured lesson and reinvent themselves by adapting their instructional strategies to unfamiliar situations, giving students a voice in the classroom and incorporating their students' creativity into the teaching/learning process. The deliberate absence of an answer key likewise serves to remove restrictions, promote creativity and thereby enhance enjoyment for both student and teacher.

To the Learner

IN A STRANGE LAND consists of four stories written to engage you in pleasure reading – a real-life experience where you enjoy stories written for you as a reader, rather than as a foreign or second language learner. For this reason, you should not regard this collection as just another book for classroom use.

We believe that you will find these stories attractive and engaging as they contain characters and situations that are familiar to us from our daily lives. As a result, you will be able to not only make personal connections between the texts you read and your own life experiences, but also connect the stories to other texts you may have read before. Likewise, you will have an opportunity to empathise with the characters and experience similar or completely new life situations.

The suggested activities are intended to be a motivational tool and provide excellent support for your learning. They promote co-operation, creativity and meaningful communication in the target language. Additionally, they will help you to practise English by discussing individual parts of the texts and predicting the course of events. The text will also encourage you to respond creatively to the content.

We hope you will find this volume a useful resource for your language practice and learning.

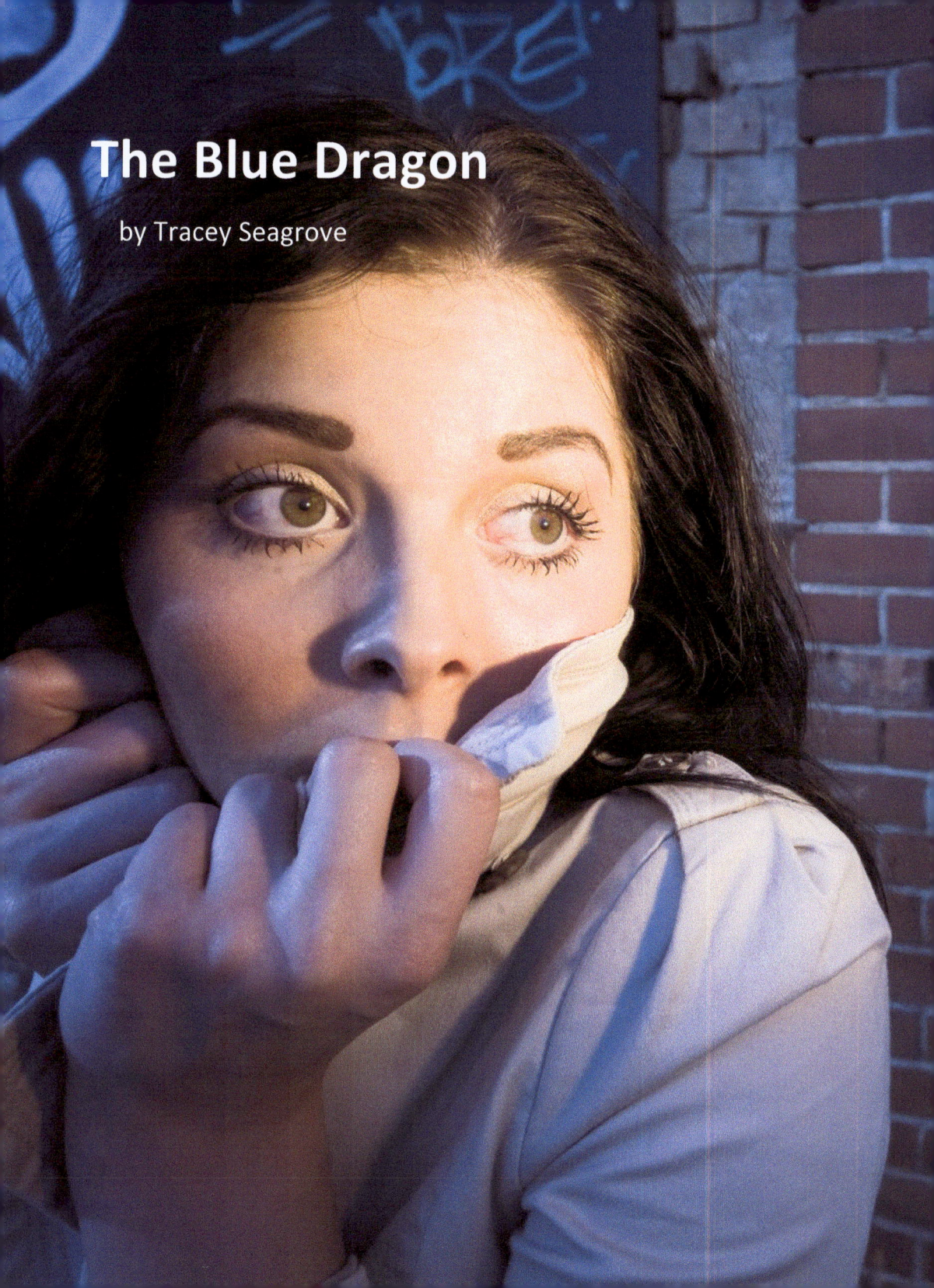

THE BLUE DRAGON

OUTLINE OF ACTIVITIES

1 **Pre-reading:** Talking about emotions
    1.1 Creating a spider diagram showing emotions and feelings
    1.2 Sharing and explaining emotions and feelings
    1.3 Group discussion and collaboration on emotions and feelings

2 **Visualising and predicting:** Focusing on the title and the opening
    2.1 Discussing and describing the blue dragon; making notes
    2.2 Identifying and discussing the characteristics of a good opening

3 **Empathising:** Understanding the language of feelings
    3.1 Identifying and expanding vocabulary to express emotions
    3.2 Creating a BEFORE and AFTER list of character development

4 **Creative writing:** Inventing a fictional character
    4.1 Becoming a character and using dialogue
    4.2 Relating characters to events; writing emails

5 **Extension and experimentation:** Making videos
    5.1 Practising and producing a video on a given topic
    5.2 Preparing and producing a video based on personal experience

— ✦ —

Sasha had not realised how dark Cambridge would be in October. The day she'd left her village home in Southern Romania, she had sat in the garden with her friends, drinking wine and talking of the future. The late afternoon sun had warmed their bodies, the light evening stretching out before them. Had it really taken only two days to move between a vibrant place where everything and everyone was familiar, to a land so grey and alien?

She focused on the paper in her hand. The address was for a hall of residence. She was on the correct street and needed to find the right building. There were several and they all looked the same. Modern, purpose-built flats, at odds with the traditional buildings of the university. She tried to forget the feelings of loneliness and isolation and concentrate on her good fortune. A chance to study in one of the best places in the world. She remembered her mother's words when she received her scholarship. 'You have always been the bright one. Go. Make the world your own. Make us proud.'

It was a dream. She had been swept up in the excitement of telling her friends. Watching their excitement and jealousy, she enjoyed both. Those last few weeks at home had flown by in a flurry of parties, noise and goodbyes.

Sasha wished her friends were with her. Together they would laugh at the darkness and the cold. Alone, the discomfort filled Sasha's thoughts. She hadn't realised how the wind would strip away the warmth from her skin, passing through her jumper and coat as if they weren't there. It made her feel oddly naked and vulnerable. It wasn't as cold as the winters back home but this shouldn't be winter. Not yet. October should be the time of a dying summer and mellow autumn.

The blocks of flats were in darkness, adding to the sinister feel of the area. Although there were more streetlights than at home, it felt shadowy, more threatening. The noise of traffic on the main road emphasised the quietness around her. She had never felt afraid of the dark before. Her mother had once caught her sneaking out at night to go swimming with some friends. Her mother's fury had been more frightening than anything the dark could hide. Except now. Now she would gladly face her mother's anger rather than have to walk around these unfamiliar buildings.

The women who helped her sort out her accommodation, explained that the flats were mainly for students in their first year and that most of them would not be arriving for another week. Being a foreign student meant she started a few days before the others and she had wanted to arrive early to give herself time to get to know the area. That didn't seem such a good idea now. At least if there were other students, people her own age, she would have company, even if they were strangers. There would be noise and lights and people to talk to and ask questions of. She could practice her English, learn some new words, slang maybe. The type of language she couldn't learn from books and that was not taught or spoken in the classrooms of her school back home. At least they were expecting another five students tomorrow. They were all from the same country. But it was a different country from Sasha's. Everything was different.

A car turned into the street, accelerating towards her, going too fast. She turned and was blinded by the headlights as the car slowed and began to crawl along, keeping alongside her as she walked. Sasha could hear the thudding beat of music even before the window was wound down and voices jeered at her. The words were unfamiliar but the meaning was clear. There were several young men in the vehicle, their laughter mocking her. Sasha wanted to run, but she had nowhere to go. Quickening her pace, she kept her eyes focused on the pavement in front of her.

A blare of its horn and a squeal of tyres as the car sped past her. She watched as the red tail lights turned at the end of the road and disappeared. Sasha stood trying to control her breathing before turning to retrace her steps. She may have passed her flat in the last few minutes. A soft footstep sounded on the grass in front of the buildings and she screamed as a torch shone into her eyes.

'What are you doing here?' The speaker lowered the torch but not enough for Sasha to see his face.

'Excuse me. I am a student. I have a flat here.'

Sasha tried to pass the man but he stepped sideways blocking her path. She tried to keep her voice calm. 'Are you a student too?'

'Me? You must be joking. No, I'm sort of a maintenance man.'

'Excuse me?'

'You know. I fix stuff.' The man flicked the torch in an arc around him. 'I look after the grounds mainly.'

'They look well tended. Isn't it late to be gardening?'

The man shrugged. 'I fix other stuff too.'

'Well, I must be on my way. Goodbye.' Sasha waited for the man to step aside.

The man looked back over his shoulder before turning around to face her again. 'What are you doing here anyway? Bit early isn't it? Term doesn't start for another week.'

Sasha wiped her hands down her jeans; despite the cold they were sweating. She smiled. 'A group of us arrived early. We are foreign students. We came to practice our English before lectures start.'

The man stepped to one side and looked around. 'There are more of you?'

'About twenty. I was just on my way to see a friend.' Sasha waved her arm vaguely in the direction of one of the buildings.

'Bit late for socialising isn't it?'

'We have not got used to the time here.'

'Right. Well, off you go before your friend comes looking for you.'

Sasha started to walk away then she turned. The torch was now hanging loose in the man's hand. She could make out his build, his height and a tattoo on his left forearm. A blue dragon. His eyes were still in shadow but she could make out the lower part of his face. Along the line of his right jaw was a jagged scar, maybe three centimetres long. Sasha smiled. 'It was nice to meet you.'

The man turned and walked away.

At last. This was her building. She couldn't pronounce the name but the letters matched those written on her paper. She dug in her pocket for the key she'd been given. She found her room on the third floor. It was little bigger than a cupboard but managed to contain a desk, bed and shower room. It was fine as long as you didn't invite someone in or want to walk around much. Somewhere along the corridor was a shared kitchen. There would be time for that later. She sank with relief onto the bed, exhausted by the journey and by her emotions.

Waking in the darkness, Sasha took a few moments to remember where she was. There was an orange glow in the room cast by a street lamp which stood below her window. She was hungry and thirsty. In her backpack she had food bought at a shop suggested by the lady who supplied her with the address and key to her flat. Sasha had found the money difficult and had been embarrassed counting out the unfamiliar notes and coins while the queue of people waiting behind her shuffled impatiently.

Sasha opened her backpack and grabbed the plastic bag containing her groceries. She took her key and opening her door, looked along the corridor which stretched away into darkness in both directions. Ranks of doors, the same as her own, were lined along each wall until she could no longer make out their shape. Which way to go? She couldn't remember passing a kitchen on the way to her room, but then she hadn't been looking and unless the door was different from all the others she wouldn't have noticed. She stepped out, trying to be quiet, as if her presence was unwelcome, a secret somehow.

What was that? Voices? A door slamming? The sort of sounds that could only be made by other people. Sasha hesitated. She wanted company but felt shy. She hadn't checked on her appearance since she woke up and thought she was probably a mess. She was wearing jeans and trainers bought at the market back home. They were copies of the ones you could buy here with expensive labels. She had wanted to fit in; to be sure people were not looking at her and pointing. She didn't want to stand out, to be any different from the other students. It was when she went to pick up her keys from the university accommodation office she realised she hadn't quite got it right.

Her jeans didn't fit her in the way the trousers seemed to fit the other girls she passed in town. There was something unfamiliar about the way they wore their clothes. They were a tighter fit. The colours brighter, there were more scarves and vivid bands of material in their hair. In fact, her hair was a whole other problem. She desperately needed a haircut. Her long unkempt curls, admired at home, here made her feel untidy and shabby.

Unless she was going to hide for the next week, until forced into company by the first lecture of her course, she had to meet the other students sometime. Now when there were fewer people, it might be a good time to start. At least she could ask the way to the kitchen. Her stomach rumbled to remind her how hungry she was, the sound loud in the silence that had returned to the corridor.

She turned towards where she thought the sounds had come from. She was almost sure that the noises had echoed up from somewhere below her floor, but she did not know how the sound carried in the unfamiliar building. She walked to the stairwell and looked over the hand rail. Sasha was about to call out a greeting when the sound of voices, deep and rough, stopped her.

'Turn it off.'

'What?'

'The light.'

'Why? It'll be easier ...'

The sound of breaking glass. The light went out. Darkness. Then Sasha could see the dancing beam of a torch before it was focused back onto the face of a young man.

'Get that light out of my face. What's wrong with you? You said no one's due to be here until next week.'

'People can see in.'

There were two of them, both male. One sounded angry, the other, the face in the torchlight, was frightened. The angry voice issued instructions.

'Turn around!'

'What? No way. Why did we have to come here anyway?'

'Dan sent me. You never paid him. Now it's time.'

A thud followed by a soft groan. The man holding the torch put it on the floor as he bent to drag his victim towards the door. The beam lit the blue dragon tattoo on his arm, making it dance as he flexed his muscles to lift the body.

Sasha cried out, not loudly but it was enough. The torch shone into her eyes.

'Who's there?'

Sasha stepped back. She ran into her room, locking the door, and putting her chair under the door handle. She sat on her bed, all thoughts of hunger gone. She would stay awake until morning and then report to the accommodation office what she had seen. She would ask to be moved to another building. When nothing happened she began to relax her breathing returning to normal. Then she heard it. The fire doors at the end of her corridor swung open and shut and someone was bashing on the doors in her corridor. She listened as the banging came closer and closer. Then there was battering on her own door and someone was twisting the door handle. She could hear muttered swearing and the sounds receding down the corridor. Sasha didn't move.

The next day, Sasha woke with the sun coming into her room. She had slept sitting up in her clothes. Feeling terrible, she thought she had better shower and change before going out. She was also incredibly hungry.

Washed and in clean clothes, she decided to try and find the kitchen. She left her room, carrying her belongings and went in the opposite direction to the night before. In the daylight, the corridor was still dim, the only light filtering from the windows above the doors to the rooms on the south side, but it still made a difference. Sasha was no longer scared and the corridor did not look as long as it had last night. She arrived at double doors leading to another staircase. To her left was the kitchen.

Making herself coffee and toast, Sasha thought about her situation. What proof was there that she had seen anyone? Who would believe her? How could she make someone understand? They would think she had imagined it or dreamt it. Worse still, they may think she was making it up to get attention.

She didn't want to be known as the crazy foreign student, or the one who was so homesick she told stories to get noticed. At home the police could be severe on anyone who they thought wasted their time. She doubted it would be different in England.

Studying her reflection in the glass door of the oven, Sasha made a decision. Stowing her rucksack out of sight in a cupboard in the kitchen, she walked the length of the corridor to the stairwell where she had seen the man with the blue dragon tattoo. She looked around for anything that might show what had happened the night before. Signs of a scuffle, blood even. There was nothing. Her decision made, she walked into town, went into a hairdresser and asked for a short style she saw whilst flicking through a magazine.

With her hair washed and hanging wet down her back, Sasha sat still as the hairdresser picked up her long dark curls. 'Are you sure? I mean your hair is in poor condition, but we could do a lot with it. It must have taken ages to grow it this long.'

Sasha met the woman's eyes in the mirror. 'All my life. Now I want something new.'

With a shrug the woman hooked her foot round a tall stool which she pulled towards her and sat down. With a reassuring smile to Sasha, she picked up her scissors and began to cut.

Half an hour later, Sasha walked out. Her hair, still curly, bobbed above her shoulders. The hairdresser had smiled at the end result. 'Well, you wanted something new. It's lovely. You look completely different.'

'Good. Yes, really good.'

Sasha went into a café and ordered coffee. She sat in a window seat watching the crowds. There was no one she recognised. She expected as much, but she was relieved. She studied the young women, those about her own age, and looked at the shops they went into. There were two in particular which the teenagers seemed to frequent. They would go in, often in twos or threes, and come out chatting and laughing, holding bags they didn't have before.

Sasha walked to the nearest shop. Its windows displaying bright, coloured trousers and casual tops. Picking up a pair of jeans, she went in and spoke to the youngest shop assistant. 'Excuse me. I am not from England. I do not know what size will suit me.'

The shop assistant smiled. 'No problem. Let's get some styles and try them on.'

'And – and shirts?'

'You want some tops, too? This colour would look great on you.'

Sasha spent a long time in the shop, and most of her allowance for the term, but what she saw in the fitting room mirror made it worth it. Even her mother would have difficulty recognising her. She walked back towards her flat but stopped at the end of the road watching. There was a man, a gardener, working in front of her building. He paused, straightening his back and looking towards her. She pretended to search for something in her bags and crossed the road going along the main thoroughfare out of town. She mingled with the crowds on the street, refusing to look back.

That evening, Sasha was waiting across the road from her building when she saw a taxi arrive with the new students. They stood on the pavement looking about them, bewildered. Sasha approached. 'Hello. Are you looking for your rooms? Can I help? I moved in yesterday.'

They looked towards her, not quite meeting her gaze. One girl stepped forward. 'Hi. I'm Diana. We have an address but...' She looked around her and shrugged.

Sasha took the paper and smiled. 'You're in my building. I was told you were coming. We'll be neighbours. You're on the third floor too. Follow me.'

Sasha led the way up the stairs.

'This is my room. You're next door.'

Diana looked at Sasha's room.

'You left your door open. Is that wise?'

'There's nothing in there. I put my bag in the kitchen.'

Diana looked puzzled, but said nothing.

That evening the building began to feel more like home. Sasha and the new students shared a meal and watched television in the kitchen which doubled as a common room. They watched the local news and a photograph of a face appeared on the screen. It was like the face of the younger man Sasha had seen the night before, a boy really. It could be him. Could be. He had gone missing from home a couple of days before. Anyone who had seen him was asked to call the number on the screen. He was last seen in an area of town known for its students.

'Are you alright, Sasha? Do you know him?'

Sasha wiped her hands down her jeans.

'No. How could I?'

That night Sasha stayed up talking to Diana and fell asleep on her floor. She felt safer there. It was a pattern that was to be repeated, although Sasha knew it couldn't go on forever. She had seen the gardener again, but at a distance. Not up close. She wasn't ready for that yet.

Three weeks later and the rooms were all full. There was lots of noise every evening and always someone off to a party. Sasha went too, sometimes. The autumn colours on the trees were stunning. It was almost as beautiful as the forests back home. Almost. On a clear, crisp afternoon, Sasha and Diana were returning from college when Diana nudged her in the ribs.

'Don't look now, but I think the gardener fancies you.'

'What?' Sasha looked up and saw a man raking leaves from the lawn in front of her block. His sleeves were rolled up and she could see a blue dragon curling up his left forearm.

Diana giggled.

'He's coming over. Shall I leave you to it?'

'No. Don't go.'

The man stood in front of the girls, his head on one side. The light catching the scar on his jaw. He smiled at Sasha.

'Do I know you?'

'No, I don't think so.'

'I thought I saw you a few weeks ago.'

Sasha wiped her hands down her jeans.

'No. I have not been here long.' She walked past him without glancing back but heard him speak to Diana.

'Did your friend use to have long hair? Down to about her waist?'

'No,' laughed Diana. 'She has always had her hair like that. Ever since I've known her.'

As Diana caught up with Sasha she looked over her shoulder.

'He's still watching you. Why did you lie to him?'

'He gives me the creeps, that's all. I thought it would be easier.'

'He does seem a bit odd. I'd stay away from him if I were you.'

'Don't worry. He thought I was someone else. Now he knows I'm not who he wants, I don't think he'll bother me again. Let's just forget him.'

Diana held open the door to their building.

'You want to stay on my floor again tonight?'

Sasha smiled.

'No. I think I'll stay in my own bed. There's no reason why I shouldn't.'

ACTIVITY 1   Talking about emotions

1.1 How many emotions can you think of that a writer may evoke in a reader? Draw a spider diagram to name as many emotions and feelings as you can or draw facial expressions to illustrate different feelings. Complete and expand the following diagram:

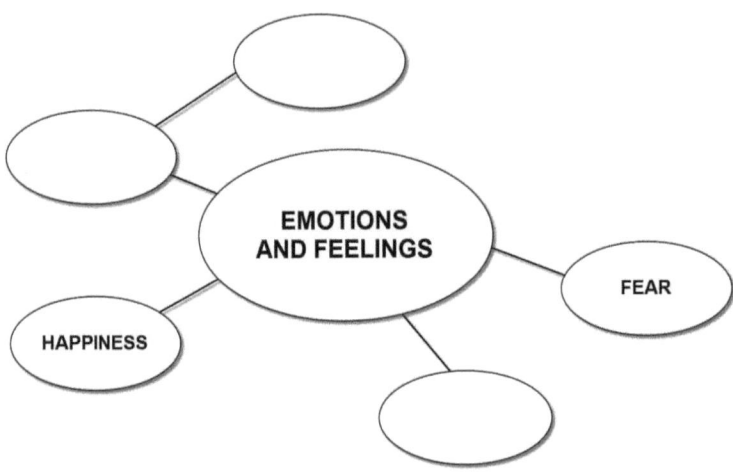

1.2 Work in pairs. Compare and share your spider diagrams. To what extent are your diagrams different? Discuss and justify the words and expressions you have each selected.

1.3 Design a class EMOTIONS and FEELINGS spider diagram with related vocabulary. Decide on the most appropriate format and medium for this diagram (poster, digital, etc.). Spider diagrams are a useful way of learning vocabulary.

ACTIVITY 2   Focusing on the title and the opening

2.1 Before reading the story, start by looking at its title. What clues does it give you about the subject of the story or the ideas it will address? How do you visualise the blue dragon? Can you draw it or describe it? What is the story about? Make notes on your ideas before sharing them with the group.

2.2 The opening of a story must be attention-grabbing to draw the reader into the story. Working with a partner, read the opening of *The Blue Dragon* and discuss:

- how the reader is drawn into the story;
- how language is used to interest or intrigue the reader;
- what information is given about the characters.

> Sasha had not realised how dark Cambridge would be in October. The day she'd left her village home in Southern Romania she had sat in the garden with her friends, drinking wine and talking of the future. The late afternoon sun had warmed their bodies, the light evening stretching out before them. Had it really taken only two days to move between a vibrant place where everything and everyone was familiar, to a land so grey and alien?

ACTIVITY 3   Understanding the language of feelings

3.1 Read the following extract from the story and identify the feelings and emotions the character is experiencing. Then go back to your spider diagram in Activity 1 and add any feelings you find in the extract. List the words the writer uses in the text to create each emotion.

For example: happiness — sat in the garden with her friends
parties and noise, …

> Sasha had not realised how dark Cambridge would be in October. The day she'd left her village home in Southern Romania she had **sat in the garden with her friends**, drinking wine and talking of the future. The late afternoon sun had warmed their bodies, the light evening stretching out before them. Had it really taken only two days to move between a vibrant place where everything and everyone was familiar, to a land so grey and alien?
>
> … She tried to forget the feelings of loneliness and isolation and concentrate on her good fortune. A chance to study in one of the best places in the world. She remembered her mother's words when she received her scholarship. 'You have always been the bright one. Go. Make the world your own. Make us proud.'
>
> It was a dream. She had been swept up in the excitement of telling her friends. Watching their excitement and jealousy, she enjoyed both. Those last few weeks at home had flown by in a flurry of parties, noise and goodbyes.

3.2 Create a BEFORE and AFTER list to compare the ways in which Sasha changes over the course of the story. Compare and discuss your lists in small groups.

BEFORE	AFTER
She had never felt afraid of the dark before	…it felt shadowy, more threatening

ACTIVITY 4   Inventing a fictional character

4.1 Imagine you could become a new character in the story. Decide with a partner:

- when you would like to appear and why
- what kind of relationship you would have with Sasha or any other character
- how your behaviour would influence the course of events

Then write a dialogue between you and the chosen character and insert it in the story. You may need to make some changes in the original text so that your dialogue is well-integrated with the rest.

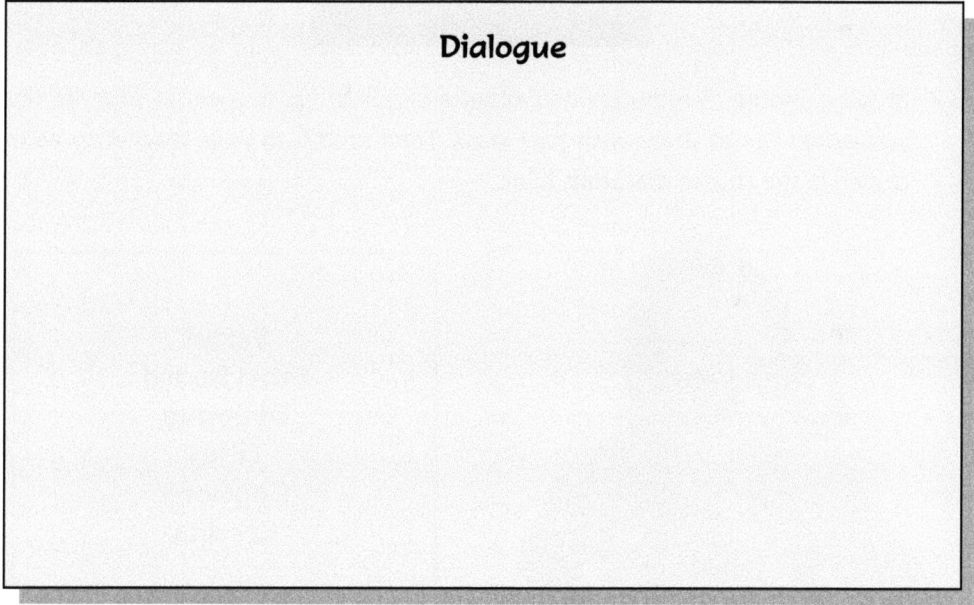

Dialogue

4.2 Produce a series of emails between one or two of the characters about the events of the story and send them to someone in your group. Be ready to reply to any email you may receive.

ACTIVITY 5 Making videos

5.1 Imagine you are Sasha. You want to share your Cambridge experience with other students. Produce a 3-minute video. Practise with a partner in order to keep the timing and produce a recording.

5.2 Prepare another 3-minute video about an interesting moment in your life that you would like to share with your class. Then send it to your teacher to be included in the course materials bank.

Script
Storyboard
Dialogue
Titles
Captions
Credits

Lights...
Camera...
Action!

THROUGH WALLS

OUTLINE OF ACTIVITIES

1 **Pre-reading:** Talking about meaning, effect and context
   1.1 Approaching the story through the title
   1.2 Approaching the story through key words
   1.3 Lexical fields – expanding vocabulary
   1.4 Studying words in context and explaining meaning

2 **Engaging with the text:** Analysing and discussing specific aspects
   2.1 Reading for detailed information
   2.2 Presenting the main character and setting the mood
   2.3 Writing a description of the main character

3 **Exploring the story:** Making connections
   3.1 Answering questions and relating to fictional characters
   3.2 Classifying words and phrases in order to understand the story

4 **Extension and experimentation:** Sequencing events and developing the story
   4.1 Explaining metaphors
   4.2 Plotting the development of events in a diagram
   4.3 Writing an epilogue to the story
   4.4 Reading aloud – pronunciation and intonation
   4.5 Reflection on how to improve writing

— ༄༅ —

It's started again. The man's voice loud and hard against the wall. The sound of furniture being dragged across the floor. A crash of a plate or a cup breaking on the floor. I can't hear her, though. I know she's in there, but she is silent.

We had only been living in this room for a few days when I first heard the noises. It always happened during the day. It was quiet at night. My parents go out to work and I haven't started school here yet, so I was always here on my own. I tried to tell them about it.

My father said, 'Don't be so sensitive, son. People are different here.'

'But what if he's hurting someone,' I said.

He said, 'You don't know that; you should mind your own business.'

'Listen to your father,' my mother said. 'We don't want any trouble.'

Then my father stopped me talking about it. 'What have I told you?' he said. 'I want to hear you speaking only English. It is our language now.'

So then I had no words.

My father came here before my mother and me. He knows some English and he changed his name. When I arrived, he changed mine too. I am John now. It feels wrong in my mouth. He says that it will make it easier for me to fit in. I don't think I will ever fit in. He says that things will be better when I start school. I don't think they will. I am too old to start learning things in a new language. I told my father I should just go to work like him.

'Don't be so stupid,' he said. 'You want to do more than drive a taxi, don't you? And you can't even learn to drive here yet. What would you do?'

My mother doesn't need to speak English. That's what my father says. She doesn't need it for her work.

'And,' he said 'You will learn English and help her.'

My mother smiled at me. She believed this story.

The schools have been on summer holidays, but it has been a strange summer. It rained all the time for weeks. I sat in our room wearing both of my jumpers and watched the rain. That's how I first saw her. I was looking out of the window at the rain falling into puddles on the pavement. Two small puddles were growing closer together, about to join up to become one huge puddle. Our window is above the front door of the house where we have our room. I heard it opening and saw her. I saw her head from above. She had blue hair. I had never seen anyone with blue hair. It was bright blue as though it had been washed in ink. I stared. She was skinny. She wore jeans and a T-shirt. Her white arms were bare and wrapped round her body. They looked to be no more than bones. She stood on the front step. She looked up and down the street and seemed to sway, preparing to move but not moving, like a cat.

Then I heard a shout from the room next door and the door opening. Running feet thumped down the stairs. I leant my face against the window to see what was happening below. Two thick hairy arms grabbed at the girl and pulled her inside. I heard feet stumbling back up the stairs and the sound of something being dragged back into the room next door. Then there was shouting.

We have a small television in our room and my father told me to watch it. 'It'll help with your English,' he said. In many of the programmes there is a lot of shouting. People with their faces screwed up spitting words at each other. I imagine their faces when I listen to the sounds from the other room. Something in the voice of the man next door is worse. It is deeper, colder, more like a punch. Usually the girl shouts back, sharp like sparks from a fire. His voice smothers hers and then there is silence. This is how it usually goes, but today the girl is silent.

After I saw the girl, I couldn't stop thinking about her and her blue hair. It was short but it stuck out in soft spikes, like the mane on the toy lion I had back home. I am much too old for toys now, so it was left behind. My lion's mane had been a golden brown colour, not blue. Nothing I had ever seen had blue hair.

The room I live in with my parents has two beds, a small table with three chairs, a wardrobe and a chest of drawers. There is a small kitchen area with a sink and a small electric oven. My mother hates it.

'I can't cook food for a family on this,' she said.

'It won't be forever,' my father said.

How long is not forever?

There is no bathroom. We have to use a bathroom shared with the other rooms on our floor. There was us, the man and the girl with blue hair and an old man. The old man coughs like he's going to die and you can hear him spitting into the toilet even from our room. The bathroom always smells if you go in after him. I take a deep breath outside and try not to breathe again before I come out.

At the start, I tried not to go to the bathroom when anyone else was around. I would listen at our door until everything was quiet, open it just a little to check the corridor was empty and then rush there and back as quickly as I could.

After I'd seen the girl with the blue hair, things changed. I started listening to hear her footsteps in the corridor. The old man shuffled like his shoes were too big and he couldn't lift his feet. The man next door slammed the door of his room and walked heavily, so it felt as though the whole floor moved under his weight. The girl was light and quick. I had to listen hard not to miss her coming and going. I started to open our door, just a little, so I could see a narrow view of the corridor and see her slip through it. One day she looked straight at me. Her eyes were blue like her hair. They shot ice at me. They said, 'What are you looking at? What do you want? How dare you look at me?'

Still, I kept watching. I sat on the floor by our door and watched the corridor until my legs hurt and my whole body was stiff. The old man went to and from the bathroom about once an hour. Every Wednesday a woman came and mopped the floor with dirty water. I noticed that the room next door was the only one that had visitors. People would come up the creaking stairs and the door of the room would open before they knocked. There were men and women, sometimes alone sometimes in twos and threes. One man came every week on a Wednesday. I knew because it was the same day the cleaner came. He was tall. He wore a long leather coat and heavy boots. The girl with the blue hair would sit in the corridor while the man was in the room. I'd shut our door so she wouldn't see me, but I'd stay sitting on the floor just a metre away from her. I thought I could feel her breathing.

One day I heard the creaking on the stairs and saw a man and a woman come into the corridor. They stopped and looked around. Slowly and quietly I shut our door. Their footsteps came down the corridor, passed by the room next to ours and kept coming. I turned the key in our door just a second before the handle turned as someone tried to come in. The door was rattled and a man's voice shouted something. I stepped backwards, watching the door like it was an angry wolf that might jump at me. Then I heard the voice of the man next door and footsteps moved away. I thought I would stop watching the corridor after that and for the next few days the door stayed locked. Then I started again.

One day my father said, 'What do you do all day?' Then he said something in English I didn't understand. He said it again and again. He was angry. My mother watched. I could see she wanted me to do something, to answer. I couldn't. I didn't know what he was saying.

'I said, 'What do you do all day?' He was shouting now.

'Nothing,' I said.

'Yes,' he said. 'Nothing. You sit here all day doing nothing. You should be learning.'

He switched on the television and dragged me in front of it. He jabbed his finger at the screen and the pretty woman looking out at me and speaking words I didn't recognise. Pictures of a car blowing up, smoke, dirt, people running. It must have been the news.

'Listen and you will learn,' my father said. He went to his coat hanging on the back of the door and pulled out some papers. 'And read these.'

He threw some children's comics at my feet. Comics for little children. Bright colours and cartoon animals. I recognised one or two of the animals from television. My mother looked at me and nodded. I picked up the comics. At home I had thought I would soon be a man, but here I was a child again, a baby. I was kept inside and given children's comics. I had lost my freedom and my language. I missed my friends. I missed talking. I missed going out on the street, going to school, listening and understanding.

When my parents were about to leave the day after, my father threw one of the comics at me. He said one word. I thought the word meant 'read'. I was angry, but now I did know a word of the stupid language that flew around outside my head. Read. I sat on the floor by the door and tried to read the comic.

I found a page with a picture of a rainbow. Each stripe in the rainbow was a different colour and had a different word in the colour. One stripe was the colour of the girl's hair. I tried out what I thought were the sounds of the letters in the word. Blue.

I had started to get braver. Now if the girl looked towards our door when she passed, I didn't close it. Once I even opened it a little wider and I thought I saw her smile. Then the door of her room opened and she looked away quickly. I noticed that the girl sometimes had marks on her arms and on her face. They were bruises that changed colours over the days from red to purple to green to brown. New ones would appear before the old ones had completely faded. Still the shouting and noises came through the wall from next door.

One day I stood up when I heard her coming. I opened the door and said my word: 'blue'. She didn't seem to understand. I touched my hair and pointed at hers and then tried again. 'Blue.' She smiled, a beautiful smile, then she whispered a word that sounded the same but different to the one I had said. I had said it wrong but she had understood. She said it again and touched her head. Then we both heard the floor creak in the room next door. She looked away at her feet and I shut the door.

After that we would often meet like this, just for a moment once or twice a day. From her I learned the words for 'hello' and 'goodbye'. The first time I said the word for goodbye to my father he stopped on his way out of the door. He came back and put his hand on my head. He nodded and smiled. I started to watch television again and listened out for my words: read, hello, goodbye, blue.

One Wednesday the man in the leather coat didn't come when he usually did. It was the afternoon and the noises from next door were worse than ever. I thought I heard furniture being thrown. I heard the crack of wood as something hit the wall. Perhaps it had been a chair. I looked at our three chairs, all different shapes and colours. I heard the girl shout back. Then I heard a scream and a bump as something hit the floor. Then everything went quiet. Later I heard the man's heavy footsteps walking up and down the room. I followed the sound of his footsteps with my eyes – over towards the window, back towards the door, over and over. Just before my parents were due home, I saw the man in the leather coat through the window. He was walking towards the house. I heard the door open and heavy footsteps go quickly down the stairs. The front door opened. Looking out of the window, I could see the man in the leather coat come inside and then I heard loud talking, like an argument. I opened the door to our room, the corridor was empty and the door of the next room was open. I looked inside. It was a mess. A broken chair lay on the floor. Crouched by the door, her back against the wall, sat the girl with blue hair. Her face was red. She'd been crying. She said a word to me I didn't understand. I smiled. She shook her head and said it again looking me in the eyes, her blue eyes trying to make me understand. We both heard the footsteps on the stairs and I left.

I watched television all the time then, switching channels all the time, listening for that word she had said. I watched television in the evenings until even my father said, 'Stop that! Turn it off!' I knew he meant it because he spoke in our own language. He only did that when he really wanted me to understand something.

I watched everything: news; films; music programmes; programmes about houses and food; children's programmes. I was watching a children's cartoon about a fireman when I heard the word. I stared at the television waiting to hear it again. A child was in a house that was on fire. She was leaning out of the window and shouting the word. She kept shouting it until the fireman came and got her out of the house. 'Help.' That was what the child had been shouting and what the girl with the blue hair had said. They both needed the same thing. But what could I do?

That night I tried to talk to my father.

'I think there is a girl next door who needs help, Papa,' I said.

'Speak English,' said my father.

'I can't...' I said.

'You have to,' he said.

'Not now, Papa. I need to tell you something.'

'I don't want to know unless you can tell me in English,' he said.

I saw my mother shaking her head at me but I had to try again.

'The man in the room next door is hurting the girl,' I said.

'How do you know? You should mind your own business. And concentrate on learning English. You start school soon.'

'Papa, I've heard him shouting at her.'

'So, you've heard a father shouting at his daughter. A father can do that to his child. And more if that child is not good and does not do as he is told.'

I had not thought of the man being her father. Where was her mother? I knew fathers could be strict, but not like this. This was wrong.

'But, Papa...'

'No,' he said. He put down his fork. 'You will mind your own business and we will not talk about this again.'

I haven't heard the girl's voice for days now. I have seen her once or twice passing the doorway, but she looks away. She seems to walk more slowly and carefully. It's Wednesday and I sit by the window looking out for the man in the leather coat. Just before noon I see him coming down the street. His coat flaps behind him like a cloak. This will be the time.

I hear his footsteps thud up the stairs two steps at a time. The door of their room opens and closes again. I walk quietly to my door and open it. The girl is sitting in the corridor with her head down and her eyes closed. She looks like a broken doll. There is a deep purple bruise all across one side of her face.

I whisper across to her: 'Blue.'

She doesn't look up. Could she be asleep? I try again.

'Hello Blue,' I say.

She opens her eyes and looks at me, but doesn't seem to see me.

'Help Blue,' I say.

She seems to wake up. She looks at the door to her room and shakes her head.

I nod and say it again: 'Help Blue.' I use my hand to show that she should come to me, come inside my room. 'Help Blue.'

She gets up. I can see that it hurts to move, but she has to move quickly. I reach out and pull her inside. I close the door and put my finger to my lips. A moment later the door of the next room opens. Heavy steps come out and start down the stairs but the door hasn't shut. The man, Blue's father, shouts. I look at her and she looks frightened, really frightened. I remember a dog my grandfather ran over when I was in the car with him back home. The dog stood in the middle of the road unable to move as we hit it. I saw its eyes and they looked like hers do now.

I put my finger to my lips again. We don't move. The man walks down to the bathroom. He shouts again and we hear him run down the stairs, two steps at a time. He jumps the last few steps and the front door opens. I run to the window and look around the edge of the curtain. He's standing on the front step looking up and down the street. He's coming back. His footsteps stop outside our door, then move on. I open the wardrobe and show Blue that she should get inside. I pull her arm to make her move. Down the corridor I can hear Blue's father talking to the old man. Then he comes back to our door and knocks. Checking that the wardrobe is closed, I open our door. He looks huge. He hasn't shaved and I can see every black hair on his chin. He's talking to me.

'Hello,' I say, and I smile.

He keeps talking. He uses his arm to indicate a smaller person. He points to his hair and says the word I know. I pretend not to know it and shake my head. He is getting angry but I keep smiling. Finally, he walks away and goes back into his room. I hear something like china smashing.

I open the wardrobe and she looks at me and smiles. I feel happy, happier than I have felt since we left home.

I have a plan and I have to make Blue understand what she needs to do. I have some English money that I took from my mother's purse. I will be in bad trouble if I'm found out. I put the money into her hand and then act out what we both need to do next.

First we leave the room. There is a floorboard that always squeaks and I almost tread on it. She takes my hand to stop me. Her hand feels so cold and small around my warm fingers. She goes to the stairs and starts to edge down them. When she's just out of sight, I knock on the man's door. He opens it, looks up and down the corridor and then stares at me. I start to talk. I say all the things that have been in my head over the past few weeks: how I miss home; how I can't believe how much it rains in this country; how I know what he does and why those people come to see him and never stay. He looks confused and then angry. He shakes his head at me, spins his finger around his ear to suggest that I am mad. I understand him but pretend not to. Finally, when I am sure that Blue will have had time to get away through the front door and down the street, I stop.

'Goodbye,' I say. I walk away, back to my room. I shut the door and then I do a silent victory dance like the footballers do when they score a goal.

* * * * * * * * *

The next Wednesday the man in the coat comes again as usual. I've been watching television. I'm beginning to recognise more words.

Just as I hear the man's boots coming up the stairs, I hear sirens. Out of the window I see two police cars and a van with their lights flashing. They stop and all the doors open at once. I can't count the number of uniformed police who come rushing at the front door to the house. They break the door down and then I can hear a rush of feet on the stairs and in the corridor. They break down the door to Blue's father's room and I can hear the two men shouting.

I'm still looking out of the window as Blue's father and the man in the leather coat are taken out by the police. On the other side of the road I see a parked car and in the back I see the top of a head, a head with blue hair. Part of a face appears for just a moment and a small white hand waves up at me. Hello Blue. Goodbye.

ACTIVITY 1   Talking about meaning, effect and context

1.1 The title of this story is *Through Walls*. The main character and narrator of this story lives in a room with his parents. Imagine and think about the noises and voices you may hear through the walls in your room and make a list below. Then, compare/discuss your list with two other students and update your list with interesting ideas.

	ME	PARTNER 1	PARTNER 2
NOISES	birds singing		
VOICES		neighbours talking	

1.2 The writer of this story chooses words and sentences for effect. Complete the following crossword which contains words you will find later in the story.

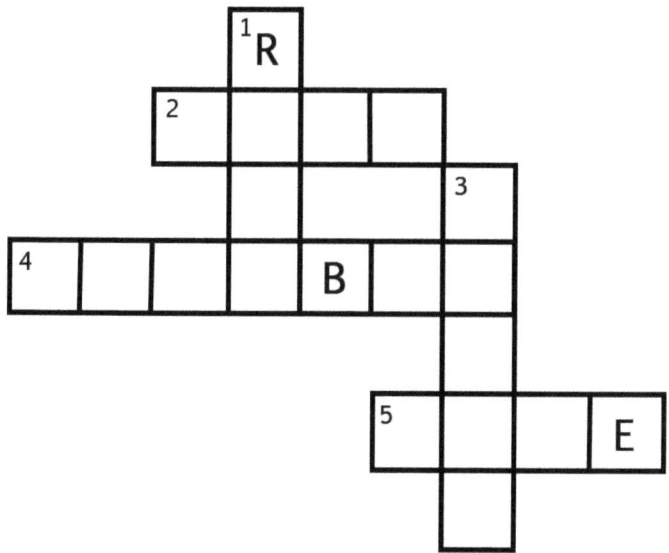

ACROSS:

2. You shout it when you are in danger in order to attract someone's attention so that they can come and rescue you.
4. People say it when they are leaving or somebody is leaving.
5. The colour of the sky in a sunny day.

DOWN:

1. The ability to look at and understand written words.
3. Greeting someone for the first time in the course of the day.

1.3 Put the scattered words in the five categories provided and explain their meaning and context of use.

skim   glance at   depressed
gloomy   scan   aid   hi there
farewell   cheers   assistance

READ	HELLO	BLUE	GOODBYE	HELP

1.4 Skim through the story and find the words from the crossword in context. Write down the sentences (the context) they have been used in. Then share the sentences/contexts you have found them in with a partner and explain the meaning of these words in the story. Do not think about their literal meaning only – read between the lines and think about how these words are linked to the events in the story.

	Word	Context	Meaning
1			
2			
3			
4			
5			

ACTIVITY 2 Analysing and discussing specific aspects

2.1 Read the first two paragraphs of the story and work with two other students to complete the box with further examples from the text.

	ME	PARTNER 1	PARTNER 2	TEXT
NOISES	birds singing			
VOICES		neighbours talking		the man's voice loud and hard
OTHER	music (radio)			

2.2 Read the same extract again.

   a. In groups of three, answer the questions below. Each student should answer one question.

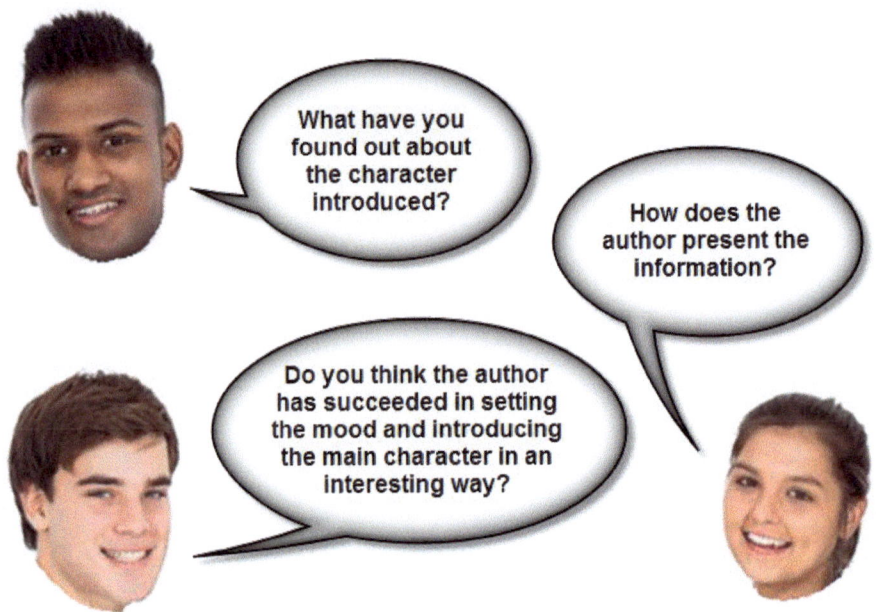

   b. Now join another group of three students and compare your answers. Evaluate the answers and choose the best ones to present to the whole class. Nominate a student to represent your group.

2.3 Skim through the first two pages of the story and on a separate sheet of paper, write a brief description of the main character. Try to use the phrases below.

    be stupid   **be different**   **be hurt**
        be silent   **be integrated into**

ACTIVITY 3 Making connections

3.1 Read the following paragraph from the story and answer the questions below.

> My father came here before my mother and me. He knows some English and he changed his name. When I arrived he changed mine too. I am John now. It feels wrong in my mouth. He says that it will make it easier for me to fit in. I don't think I will ever fit in. He says that things will be better when I start school. I don't think they will. I am too old to start learning things in a new language. I told my father I should just go to work like him.

1. What are John's reasons for learning English? How does he feel about this experience?

   ....
   ....
   ....
   ....

2. What methods of learning English are mentioned in the story? Give your opinions about them.

   ....
   ....
   ....
   ....

3. What is John's attitude towards English? What words and expressions has the author chosen and what is the effect?

....

....

....

Now reflect on your own language learning experience. Answer the following questions and post them to the class blog set up by the teacher. Feel free to write comments on others' learning experiences.

1. What are your reasons for learning English? How do you feel about this experience? Would you change your name to an English one? Would you change your nationality to British?

....

....

....

2. Have you ever tried any of the methods of learning English mentioned in the text? What methods do you prefer and why?

....

....

....

....

3.2 Most of the action in the story comes from the sounds John hears from his room. In pairs, classify the following words and phrases from the text into the following two categories: voices and footsteps / the sound of foot movement. Find the meaning of any new vocabulary in a dictionary and complete the tables below.

a shout from ... running feet thumped down
spitting words at each other ... the creaking on the stairs
I stepped backwards
loud talking, like an argument ... the sound of his footsteps
whispered a word ... a floorboard that always squeaks

Voices and footsteps	The sound of foot movement

NEW WORD	MEANING	MY SENTENCES

ACTIVITY 4 Sequencing events and developing the story

4.1 Find the moment in the story when John sees the girl with blue hair for the first time. Read it carefully and say how the metaphor in the extract below reflects the beginning of their relationship.

> I was looking out of the window at the rain falling into puddles on the pavement. Two small puddles were growing closer together, about to join up to become a huge puddle. Our window is above the front door of the house where we have our room. I heard it opening and saw her.

4.2 Work in pairs to complete the diagram below in order to Illustrate how the relationship and events develop.

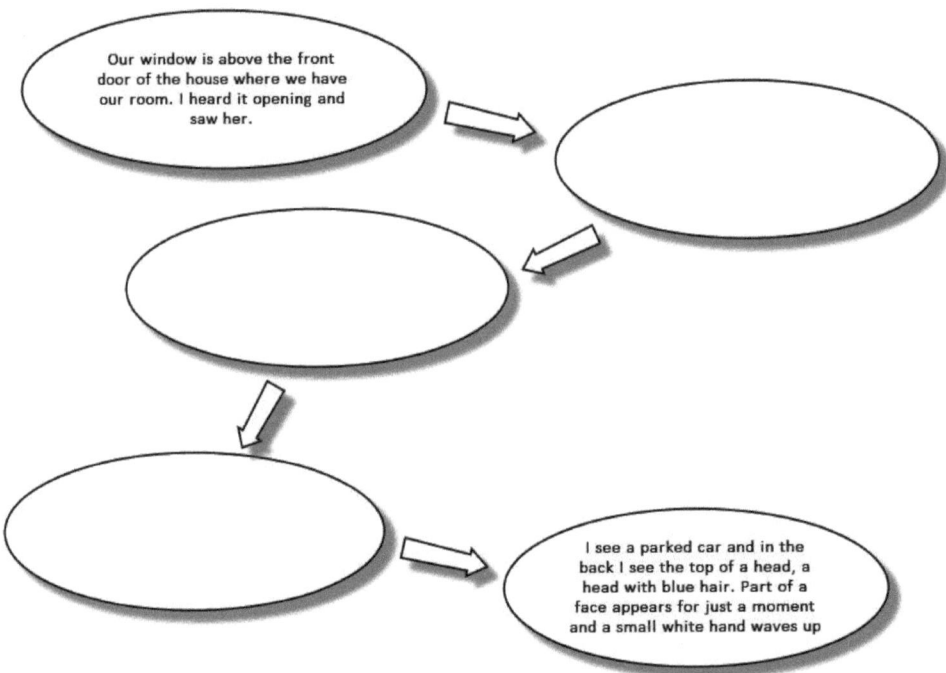

56

4.3 In pairs, write an epilogue in which you explain what happens to the characters next. An epilogue is placed at the end of a book commenting on or concluding the story. Choose the tense and tone you think is appropriate; use interesting vocabulary and engage the reader. Your epilogue should not be longer than 150 words.

4.4 Decide which of you will read your epilogue to the rest of the group. Practise your reading; check your pronunciation and intonation. Try to use your voice to convey various feelings. At the end of the lesson, the group can vote to choose the best ending for the story.

Voting card - Best Ending

1..

2..

3..

4.5 Having listened to different epilogues, write three things you plan to include in your future writing to make it better.

1 ....

2 ....

3 ....

Don't Go In

by Hannah C. Floyd

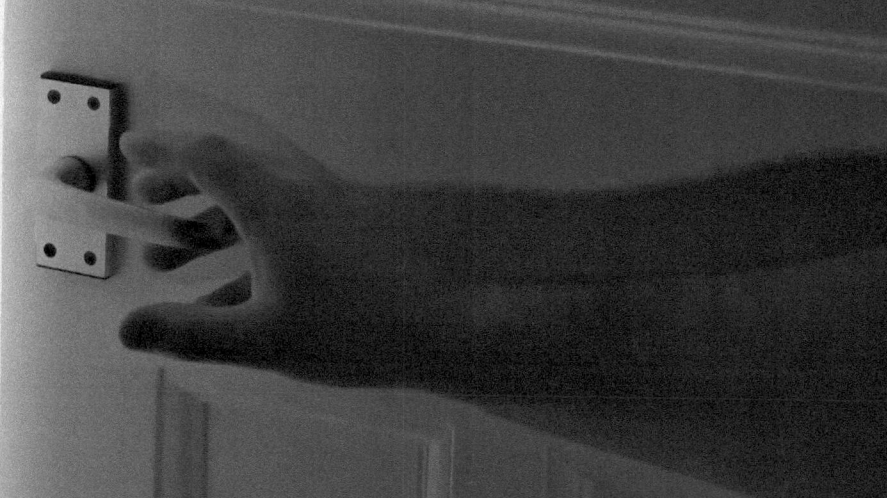

DON´T GO IN

OUTLINE OF ACTIVITIES

1 **Pre-reading:** Discussing first impressions

2 **Expressing emotions:** Understanding and using similes
   2.1. Analysing behaviour in order to understand emotions
   2.2. Finding and explaining similes
   2.3. Using similes to make writing more vivid

3 **Thinking beyond the text:** Interpreting dreams:
   3.1. Extrapolating on an episode
   3.2. Comparing dreams and reality
   3.3. Interpreting images and symbols

4 **Improvisation:** Reporting problems on the phone

5 **Experimentation:** Creating a television programme and writing a letter
   5.1. Speaking about travel
   5.2. Writing letters to a travel agent

6 **Extension:** Designing a movie poster

— ∽∾ —

I spent a bad night tossing and turning. I don't sleep well in strange beds as a rule, but this bed was definitely not for sleeping on. It was hard, with a bounce to it that made it unstable without being comfortable. The air-conditioning machine was above the bed and I couldn't find the remote to turn it down, so I shivered under the single nylon sheet – I missed my fluffy duvet with the Cars cover.

I woke several times in the night, hearing a strange shuffle-hiss-clump, coming from somewhere in the ceiling. It repeated itself for just long enough to make me wake up, then stopped. So I lay there, jet-lagged, wishing I'd brought some kind of world adaptor for my phone charger. If I could charge my phone, I'd be able to drown out any further noises with hip-hop.

Four irritating thoughts rotated on an endless loop in my mind, like abandoned suitcases on a baggage reclaim belt. They ran as follows:

1) What was I doing here? I got on the plane alright. I tried to think back to what the plane had been like, and came back with: nothing special. The connecting flight was rather floral, and the air hostesses were very neatly presented, but I'd expected Asia to be different. It was when I got off the plane and into passport control that things had started to look odd. The faces of the security guards - as if they were sharing a private joke about me. The weird, low lighting. No 'Welcome to Vietnam'. I hadn't seen a single sign, a single map. There was one taxi outside the airport. Driven by a man who looked like an elephant. No questions, just drove me to this hotel. Did I get on the wrong plane? Did I make a mistake in the student travel office? Did someone screw up when they were booking my ticket? Nothing seemed right since I got off that plane.

2) How was I going to survive? This hotel was $20 a night and I only had £500 in the bank. How long was it possible to go without food? Should I try to find a cheaper place? Maybe I could get a job? But what if this wasn't the kind of place where a foreigner could just rock up and demand a job? Would I have to get some kind of social security certificate? A work permit? Or even (I shuddered) learn the language?

3) I was suffering from severe Internet withdrawal symptoms. If I couldn't get online within the next twenty-four hours, I was worried my entire social network might come crashing to the ground.

I woke for good around six a.m. by the alarm clock next to my bed. It was already light. I decided to get out of the hotel as soon as possible and get to know the area. But first, I needed to get online to let people know I'd arrived safely.

I stood at the entrance desk, waiting to ask about the Internet. Even at six a.m., it was the hottest, humidest weather I had ever experienced. I longed for some sort of fan, or even just a breath of air from a fridge. There was no queue, just a general confusion. Nobody would meet my eye – it seemed they were doing something very important. Possibly the two people behind the desk were just asleep sitting upright.

'Excuse me, d'you know where can I get Internet access here?'

The male receptionist smiled and nodded, blankly. I tried again.

'Internet?'

His small, round face was flooded with understanding. 'Oh, Internet very easy. Just go down the road, straight, right, left, right.'

I thanked him and walked out of the hotel into the early morning smog. I started walking slowly down the street, trying not to get killed.

Pink buses with crazy paintings all over them. Bicycles with lights like eyes. Several types of motorcycle. Old men in semi-robotic rickshaws, bearded men riding giraffes - or were they camels? - dark-windowed cars, beggars on

skateboards, kids on pogo-sticks, street sellers in flip-flops: all manner of moving traffic was clogging up the road. The place was terrifying.

'You buy me chewbacca,' said a tiny girl in a green tunic which barely reached her knees. 'You buy me.'

Dunno what I was thinking when I reached into my jeans pockets. I usually say 'no' to beggars: it's like a reflex. Drew out my wallet. There were just three English 50p pieces in it, and a few five dollar bills.

She was standing there and looking at me with these huge green eyes. Her eyelashes were so dark that she looked as if she were wearing eyeliner.

I gave her the coins and she handed me a tiny clear bag, then she ran away across the impossible road, afraid I would change my mind. I slipped it into my pocket, feeling as if I'd seen some kind of ghost.

I decided to walk along the pavement till I found something familiar. A metal hand-cart was parked in the pedestrians' way. Then I had to pick my way through a fish-market spread over the pavement from a huge covered zone nearby, with metal bowls of half-dead fish and baskets of trussed-up crabs. I tried not to look at the fish, step in the blood or breathe in through my nose. A saleswoman – possibly half-fish herself – gave my leg a strong squeeze as I passed.

Thinking I'd do better off the pavement, I advanced into the road and got engulfed in a cloud of smoke. A huge truck nearly knocked me flying, and I returned to the kerb. I found myself at a stall serving fruit juices.

The stall was on the pavement in a group of tiny plastic stools. People drank tea from thimbles and chatted. The juice-vendor squeezed two hairy fruit, threw in some sugar and a scoop of ice, and passed me the dripping glass. I thanked her, and sucked it all up in one go. I felt much, much better. I could still see the sign for BIG NICE HOTEL, about a hundred metres away. It occurred to me to go back and try to make it the whole way later, maybe tomorrow. Perhaps I didn't need to use the Internet after all.

But just before I decided to call it a day, I saw a turning on the right and a sign saying: 'INTERNET'. I followed the signs and turned finally into a tiny alley with an entrance decorated with hanging jungle plants. I parted the plants and stepped into a cool, whitewashed interior. Lamps in pods lighted my way up the stairs.

I received a token with an access key from the ghostly person who was sitting at the kiosk, and sat at one of the numbered grey, hot machines. Nineteen other kids were sitting there, quietly clicking away at World of Warcraft. Facebook first. I opened my news feed. Sighed. A bird in a hanging basket started singing loudly. No news. No emails. It was as if my online life had been frozen in time. I wondered if the Internet actually connected as far as here or not. I wrote an optimistic email to Mum, saying arrived safely and everything OK.

As I sat staring at the screen, something warm brushed against my foot. There was a cat under the computer desk, looking straight at me.

'Hello Fraser,' it said, and slipped between my feet. As it jumped up to the high windowsill and slipped out, I noticed something odd about it. It had two tails.

I returned slowly to the hotel, shocked by my morning's exploration. After the outside world, my room was a safe haven. Nothing was out of the ordinary about it at all: everything was clean, ironed and arranged at right-angles. It was a small room with yellow tiled floor and plastic windows. The room was divided from the bathroom by a sliding door which I particularly liked. My open rucksack leant against a small glass coffee table by the window. A couple of mosquitoes lurked in a corner by a pot plant.

I looked out of the window. Same deadlocked traffic jam outside, creeping along and honking, and pavements full of street hawkers – what were they selling? I decided to have a long shower, forget about the cat, and try and get back to sleep. I was jet-lagged to hell. Maybe the whole thing was a product of my overtired mind.

A few minutes later, I was lying in my boxer shorts on the bed, allowing the air-conditioner to fan me dry. I closed my eyes.

No, I couldn't sleep. Something else was wrong.

Something was moving under the bed.

I immediately reached for my jeans and pulled them on. Armed with my belt, I slowly pulled back the quilt. Peered in, but could see only blackness, and a few balls of fluff.

'Come out with your arms up,' I said. 'You know who's the boss.'

Under the bed there was a deep pit. At the bottom, among some scuffling rats, was a bundle of rags which did not look right.

It bothered me, that bundle. Even more than the rats. It could have been just another bundle of rags, but it was not a natural shape for a bundle of rags. Longer. Less bunched together. I went and stood, half-dressed, in the middle of the room. Oddly, now I was a few metres away I couldn't smell the pit's mushroomy, cold air.

I let the belt drop to the ground. I needed to think. I opened the minibar, examined its contents (beer and water, mainly) and took out a can named Orange Craze. I sat in the small chair next to the coffee table and drank slowly. Something was wrong with that bundle. Rats are scary, but bundles can contain the unknown.

I picked up the phone and dialled zero, guessing that it would take me through to reception.

'Hello?'

'There's a problem with my room.'

'What room number, please?' I looked at the key fob in the ashtray on the coffee table.

'Room 103.'

'How can I help you?'

'I don't suppose you could come up here and help me deal with it?'

'I'm sorry; could you repeat that, please?' I identified the key pieces of information.

'My room. A problem. Please come.'

'OK, OK.' The line clicked.

Outside, on the window ledge sat the two-tailed cat, licking its paws. I decided to leave the room altogether and stood outside in the tiled corridor, waiting.

The corridor was too long, I decided. It must have been longer than the building. And bleak, just tiles and strip lighting all the way along. Not my idea of a hotel, really – it could have belonged to a prison.

At that point, the timer switch on the light in the corridor must have gone out, because I was plunged into blackness. I slid down the wall and sat on my butt, wondering what to do. Wondering if room service was ever going to come. The corridor was hot and stuffy in comparison with my room, and I felt sweat - or mosquitoes - start to prickle on my forehead. It was kind of unfair. This was not how a backpacker holiday should be. I crawled back into the room and sat against the door, my heart thumping. At least I could still see in here by the light from the window, though the air conditioner had stopped working. I wondered if it was a power cut.

'Whenever you're ready.'

The voice came from under the bed.

I tried to ignore it. Beds don't talk. Neither do bundles under beds.

'The fact is, you're wanted here. They want you here. It might not be in the right place or at the right time for you, but it's right for us.'

'Are you talking to someone on the phone down there?' I asked aloud. The two-tailed cat, now parading herself on the coffee table, turned her head towards me suddenly.

The bed was silent. I willed for room service to come. It didn't.

Finally, I walked over to the bed and pushed it away from me, propelling it into the partition with the bathroom and leaving the pit exposed like a wound in the floor.

At the bottom of the pit was a bundle. It had changed position since I looked in before. I stepped down into the pit: the rats had hidden themselves somewhere. Carefully, belt in hand again, I approached. A mummy? A corpse? With fingertip and thumb, I pulled back a layer of rags. It was a face - not dead but sleeping. One finger rested in his mouth as if he'd been chewing it. A paper bag lay beside him. He was mixed-up-looking: half-punk, half robot. His hair (bright orange in colour) was a squashed Mohican, now more of a Z-shape. His face was masked with metal, except for the soft lips and one closed eye.

'Can you just press on my neck?'

'Huh?' I asked.

'There's a spot just above my clavicle. Down a bit - there. Harder, please.'

I pressed. The hard plating of his metal neck gave way to my touch at that spot. I worried it would hurt him.

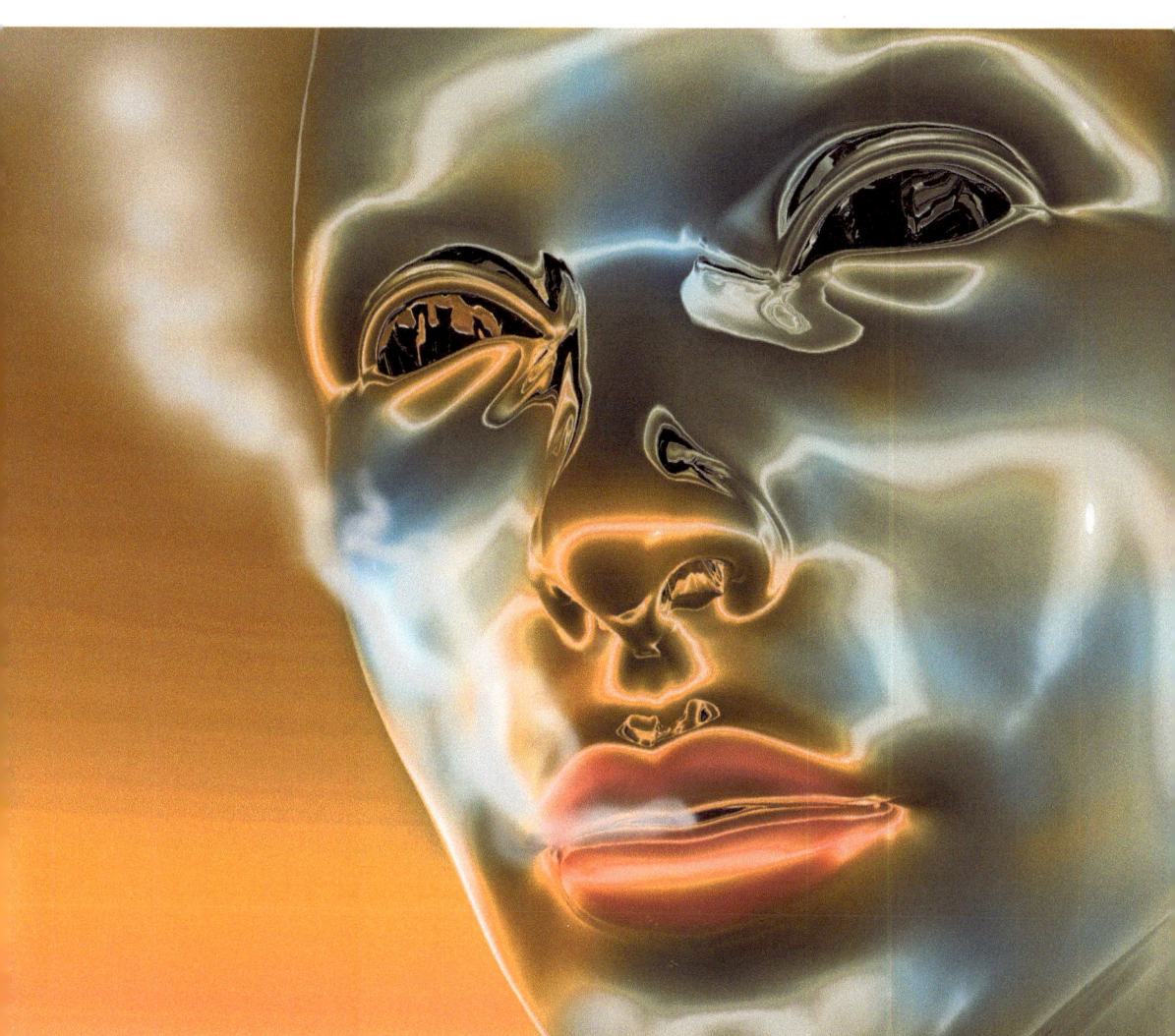

He moved. He began to twitch his fingers and face. Opening his mouth like a baby, he reached for the paper bag and started pulling it towards his lips. He took a big draw from the bag, and exhaled with a noisy series of clicks.

'Welcome. Welcome, Fraser,' he said, opening his eyes to reveal orange irises. Half his mouth smiled.

'What are you?' I asked.

'Pure craving,' he said.

'How did you get under my bed?'

'I wanted to.'

'But how?'

'Oh, through the door of your mind.'

'Well, that makes sense,' I said in annoyance. Kneeling by him like a paramedic in an emergency, I felt irritation rise up in me that he hadn't shown any surprise or gratitude towards me. How did he know my name? This place was either some weird dream I was having before getting on the plane, or I'd died in a plane crash and this was now the afterlife. How dare they put a cyborg under my bed? Who was organising this anyway? And couldn't they take pity on me and put the electricity on again please?

The cyborg sat up.

'What kind of place is this?' I asked the room.

'It's not exactly a place, to be precise,' said the cat.

I looked at the cat. It was rubbing itself against the coffee table.

'Go on,' I said.

'It is called, by some, the Little World. Not many dare say its name, for it is a fragile thing formed of notions, words, data. You might call it a phenomenon,' said the cat. She pronounced it slowly, syllable by syllable.

I think that's roughly what the cat said. I just nodded as if I understood.

The cyborg got painfully to his feet. His body was largely robot, made up of thin metal poles, his hips barely covered by a pair of cut-off jeans. Something about this guy was surprisingly ordinary, despite his appearance. He stepped out of the pit and came up to shake hands with me. I pulled my hand back suddenly, then felt bad for being rude.

'I'm Eddy,' he said.

'What are you? And why were you under my bed?'

'I was tired and needed a rest. 'Tisn't good to ask too many questions,' said Eddy. 'Let's go.'

'Where?' I asked.

'Into the door.'

'What door?' I asked.

'The one in the pit.'

'No,' I said. I didn't even look to see if there was a door there. 'That's the stupidest idea I've heard in my whole life.'

Eddy raised his orange eyebrow. Saying nothing, he sat at my coffee table, crossed his ankles awkwardly and drew a packet of cigarettes out from between two of his metallic ribs. The body language (if you can call it a body) was saying, 'I've got all day.'

I stood watching him, unsure what to do. The cat was in the pit, sniffing after rats. I didn't much feel like staying in this room any longer. Didn't feel like walking out into the dark corridor, either, or going outside. Definitely not outside. I decided that I was going mad.

'You'll never know what's in it if you don't look. And that's going to bother you, I think,' said Eddy quietly, exhaling smoke through both sides of his half-metal mouth.

On the other hand, I said to myself, the pit contained the unknown.

'It's not really a choice. Your sole purpose here is to go into the pit. The pit's sole purpose is for you to go in it. Why else d'you think it's there?'

'You're talking rubbish,' I said. I sat down on the displaced bed. 'Complete rubbish. You can go wherever you like. I don't have to go with you.'

There was a long pause. He lit another, and practised blowing smoke rings. The cat went to sleep in a patch of sunlight in the middle of the room.

At last, he said mildly, 'Well, then.' Didn't move.

I pulled on my tee-shirt, zipped up my rucksack, slipped my toes into my sandals and went to the door. I had almost closed the door when I thought better of it, and opened it enough to take one last look at the scene.

I closed the door.

The corridor was light again. The receptionist was walking along it towards me.

'Sir, very sorry for delay. We have room for you on higher floor.'

'Thank you,' I said.

The new room was 303, directly above my old room. It was oddly identical to the previous room. The pot plant was slightly different (I couldn't be sure it was real) and the bathroom door had a large crack in the acrylic partition. Apart from that, it was the same.

'Key is on the coffee table,' announced the receptionist abruptly, and closed the door. I wondered if I was supposed to tip him. Then I remembered that he should be grateful to me for not making a fuss about the pit under my bed.

I put my rucksack on the floor and lay down on the bed. Same bouncy, unsquashy mattress. The air-conditioning blasted down onto my face, relaxing me and reminding me of beautiful cool air at home. I missed Mum. I even missed my Gran.

Then, as I lay there, I remembered Eddy. A glittering, mysterious cyborg slumped in the chair next to the coffee table, smoking and staring into space. I'd never seen a cyborg, and never imagined they might smoke. What was I thinking? I was so sure I wanted to live on the wild side. But when I got the chance, I just closed the door.

Then I heard a scratching, scuffling sound.

ACTIVITY 1 Discussing first impressions

1.1 Before reading or listening to the story, read its title and look at the following images. With a partner, discuss which image might reflect the story. What could this story be about? What characters do you think you are going to encounter in the story? Do you think the title is a message you could find somewhere? Where?

Characters?　　　　　　　　　　**Where?**

　　　　　　　　Plot?

　　　　Emotions?　　　　　　　　**Message?**

Who?　　　　　　　　　　**When?**

What?

ACTIVITY 2 Understanding and using similes

2.1 Read the first two paragraphs of the story and identify two or three phrases that describe how the main character was feeling. Then, briefly explain the effect of these phrases on setting the scene in the story. Exchange your notes and views with a partner.

   1. *tossing and turning* **means the character could not sleep and he might have felt uncomfortable** ....

   2. ....
   ....

   3. ....
   ....

   4. ....
   ....

2.2 Find examples of similes in the story and explain their meaning. An example of a simile from the story is given below:

> *Four irritating thoughts rotated on an endless loop in my mind, like abandoned suitcases on a baggage reclaim belt.*

> Write your examples here

2.3 Use the simile list below to describe a funny incident from your life (150 to 200 words). Use as many similes in your description as possible. Read your description to a partner and then put it on the board for everyone to read.

as delicate as a flower	as big as an elephant	as wise as an owl
as flat as a pancake	as busy as a bee	as pale as a ghost
as free as a bird	as hairy as an ape	as stubborn as a mule
as cunning as a fox	as happy as a lark	as sharp as a razor
as cool as a cucumber	as sweet as honey	as sick as a dog
as blind as a bat	as tall as a giraffe	as cold as ice
as bright as the sun	as white as snow	as slow as a tortoise

....

....

....

....

....

....

....

....

....

....

....

ACTIVITY 3   Interpreting dreams

3.1 Read the episode when the narrator meets Eddy, the cyborg, under his bed before the receptionist comes to let him know that another room is ready for him.

> I decided to have a long shower, forget about the cat, and try to get back to sleep. I was jet-lagged to hell. Maybe the whole thing was a product of my overtired mind. A few minutes later, I was lying in my boxer shorts on the bed, allowing the air-conditioner to fan me dry. I closed my eyes.
> …
>   'Sir, very sorry for the delay. We have a room for you on a higher floor.'
>   'Thank you,' I said.

In pairs, discuss the following questions:

1. *Do you think this was a dream? Why?*
2. *What evidence is there in the text of reality and dream?*
3. *Do you often dream? Can you describe one of your weirdest dreams?*
4. *Do you think dreams have some connection with reality? How?*

3.2 Look at the five images on the next page and read the story carefully to find them in the text. Then, working in pairs, decide what sort of interpretation you could give each of the images in order to analyse the dream. Present your interpretations to the rest of the class to vote for the best or most original interpretation.

3.3 Work in pairs to research the interpretations of the images online and find out how close you were to the interpretations given by experts. You score 1 point for an accurate interpretation. Compare your scores with other pairs.

Here are some sites that might help you:

dreammoods.com   dreamtation.com
dreamingthedreams.com dreamhawk.com
dreamdictionary.org   dreamforth.com

ACTIVITY 4   Reporting problems on the phone

Read the section from page 66 – 68 indicated below:

> I returned slowly to the hotel, shocked by my morning's exploration. After the outside world, my room was a safe heaven.
> …
> 'I'm sorry; could you repeat that, please?' I identified the key pieces of information.
>
>   'My room. A problem. Please come.'

Now pretend you are the character in the story. Report the problems in your room to one of your classmates, acting as the receptionist. Use some of the information from the text as well as add extra information to make your conversation more informative and/or entertaining. Sit back to back with a classmate to simulate the telephone conversation.

ACTIVITY 5 Making a television programme and writing a letter

5.1 Work in groups of six. You are going to simulate an early morning television programme which interviews people about their holiday choices and experiences. Before you begin, decide on a name for your programme, then decide which of the following roles the members of the group will play:

Producer
Producer's assistant
Interviewer
Three interviewees

- The producer keeps control and decides when each segment (introduction, interview, group discussion, final words) is finished and gives hand signals to the interviewer (slow down, speed up, move on, wind up, etc.)
- The producer's assistant keeps a detailed record of each of the interviewees' experiences.
- The interviewer asks questions and guides the discussion.
- The interviewees talk about their experiences.

Now act out the interviews, including both positive (holidays from heaven) and negative (holidays from hell) experiences. Make notes like the example below.

HOLIDAYS	WHO	WHERE	WHY	WHEN
from HEAVEN	Marie	Barbados	Sea, food, people	2 years ago
from HEAVEN				
From HELL				
from HEAVEN and HELL				

5.2 After the interviews, choose one of the options above and write either a letter of complaint or a thank-you letter to your travel agent. As a group, decide what information you want to include and how you want to structure your letter. Proofread the letter and then exchange letters with another group. Write a reply to the letter you have received.

(Sender)

(Addressee)

Dear ....

I am writing to ....

ACTIVITY 6 Designing a movie poster

Work in groups of four and produce a poster for a film adaptation of the story "Don't Go In". You may introduce as many changes or modifications to the story or characters as you like. Present the final product to the class. In your presentation, explain why you have designed the poster in a particular way.

Preparation Guidelines:

1. Look at existing movie posters on the Internet. Some examples are shown below.
2. Discuss with your partners what makes an attractive poster.
3. Decide what to include in the poster.
4. Discuss the layout of the poster.
5. Design the poster.
6. Discuss what to include in the presentation.

MERLIN

OUTLINE OF ACTIVITIES

1. **Pre-reading:** Predicting the story line
    1.1 Reading and matching magical encounters with story titles
    1.2 Predicting content from the title
    1.3 Selecting vocabulary for the story

2. **Listening and writing:** Forming and describing first impressions

3. **Expressing feelings and opinions:** Posting comments on a blog

4. **Improvisation:** Acting out a court-room drama

5. **Creative writing:** Producing a haiku

6. **Extension:** Discussing opinions found on an internet forum

— ❧ —

I am about to tell you a story that has both mystery and magic in it, but I must, as my English teacher tells me, start at the beginning. There are things that you need to know about me, the person telling the story, before I begin.

First things first. I am sixteen years old and my name is Matilde. Maybe you want to know what Matilde means? Well, it is a Portuguese name meaning mighty in battle. I am not sure why Mae and Pai gave it to me, but I am happy with my name as I would like to think that if I had to fight a battle, I would be mighty.

The next thing you will need to know about me is that I am not living in my own country and the home that I left often seems very far away. And now I will tell you something of my home as writing the words down takes away some of the sadness of not being there.

I did not want to leave the house I shared with Mae and Pai and my little sister Ana. Our house is not a big house but it is in a very pretty square, the Praca da República in Sagres, which I will tell you is the most south-westerly town in the Algarve, a very beautiful part of Portugal. My parents, I am sure, were thinking of my future so decided to send me away for two years to live with my aunt and uncle in their house in a town in Suffolk. My aunt and uncle have a small bar and grocery shop. I would stay with them, help out in the shop and attend the local college to learn English.

I should have felt excited about leaving home on such an adventure; my friends said 'Matilde, you are so lucky to leave. What is there to do here? It is so boring.' But my life was lived in books so I was never bored, I loved my sister and parents and would have been happy never to leave. My name did not mean a seeker after adventure.

So now you know enough of me for the story to begin. It is like many of the fantasy stories I read as a child. It begins with a magical encounter.

Even though I was homesick, I was happy with my aunt and uncle. They had no children of their own and were more than kind to me. I worked in their shop at weekends and during the week went to the college a few streets away. At first it was difficult as I had very little English, but I made friends with a group of other Portuguese students so it became easier. My aunt and uncle said that I should try to make friends with the English girls, but somehow that seemed far too difficult. I was not interested in clothes or boys or any of the other things that took up their time. As for the boys, I was not impressed by them. The ones I met at college seemed very noisy and far too young.

On Wednesdays college finished at lunchtime and I would go to the library in the town to read books. I had soon read all the Portuguese books on the shelves so went to the children's section to find some story books in English that would be easy to read. While my spoken English was improving slowly, I was learning to read in English very quickly and it was not long before I worked my way up to the teenage section.

I loved all the old stories of knights and princesses, dragons and pirates, but the legend of Arthur and Guinevere was my favourite. I dreamt of the day when a dashing knight would come along and turn me into his princess. It might seem an impossible dream, but sixteen is a time to think that anything is possible, even a knight in shining armour galloping into your life on a white horse.

It was hot, a Saturday in June and the shop was crowded. The bell rang as the door opened for yet another customer. I was putting packets of soup out on the shelves and stopped what I was doing to stare. It wasn't that he was my idea of a knight in armour or even that at a glance he was especially good looking. It was something about him, some oddness that first drew my gaze. He looked uncomfortable but that wasn't it. It was the jet black hair and his amazingly blue eyes. My hair is dark and my eyes are brown. You expect dark hair and brown eyes, not black hair and blue eyes. His were so blue they were

startling and looking more closely I could see that yes, he was handsome, very handsome. He was dressed in jeans and a T-shirt, both were neat and clean although they looked quite shabby.

He moved over to the bottles of wines and spirits, looked up and saw me staring at him. I felt my face grow red and looked away, then a few seconds later, heard my uncle shout. Feet ran past me, the shop door, opened and slammed shut and my uncle ran past in pursuit. The boy with the black hair and blue eyes had stolen an expensive bottle of brandy.

My uncle caught him without much trouble and brought him back to the shop. Very soon the police arrived. The boy refused to speak until the police came. I had been watching him all that time. He seemed very calm, very sure of himself, not at all sorry for what he had done or frightened of what might happen to him. When the police asked him to explain himself all he would tell them was his name. He stood up tall, looked at them and said quite confidently, that his name was Merlin.

I gasped. I knew the name of course. Merlin was the magician in the stories of Arthur and Guinevere. I had imagined him an old man with a flowing white beard, but of course when he was young he would have looked just as the young boy in our shop looked. I wanted to hear why he had stolen the bottle. I couldn't believe it was because he wanted to get drunk. I had seen people who drank a lot at home in Portugal and they did not look as clean and self-assured as this boy. The police decided to take him to the police station and I stood by the door as they got ready to leave, one policeman in front of Merlin, one behind. For just a moment, as he passed, his eyes met mine.

Now you might say that I am just a silly romantic and have read far too many books, but I was certain that in that one look was centuries of knowledge. In that one look was a lifetime of pain and anxiety. In that one look was defiance, triumph even and with that one look my heart stood still.

They took him away of course and for hours afterwards I was upset. How was I to find out what had happened to him? I had no knowledge of how the law in England worked but knew enough to know that even if I went to the police station I wouldn't be told anything.

I didn't sleep and could hardly eat so was very relieved when two days later we heard what was to happen. My uncle received a letter saying that the young man was to appear in court the following Monday charged with theft. As he was only seventeen, it would be in the youth court. I asked my uncle if we could go but he thought it would be impossible. We wouldn't be allowed in. But I knew where the courthouse was and decided that I would miss a day at college. Even if I wasn't allowed in, I could wait outside and hopefully catch another glimpse of Merlin.

On the Sunday evening, I spent a long time on the Internet looking up anything I could find about Merlin, the wizard. There were many, many sites but I liked best the web site that said he was born of a mortal woman and his father was an incubus, a non-human male said to possess mortal women as they slept. From his father, Merlin inherited his supernatural powers and abilities. When grown, Merlin became an advisor to King Arthur until he was bewitched and imprisoned by the Lady of the Lake.

    I felt as though I had been bewitched. The boy, Merlin's black hair and blue eyes had haunted my waking and sleeping hours ever since I had first seen him.

* * * * * * *

It was hot. The courthouse was near the church, an old building and very big. I couldn't go inside so could only imagine how frightening the court rooms must be. I sat on a bench in the churchyard near to the court car park from where I could see the main entrance. There was a tree for shade and I decided to wait for however long it took for Merlin to appear. I had sandwiches, an apple and water for my lunch.

I didn't see Merlin go in, but at midday, suddenly he was there, coming out of the entrance. He stood for a while talking to a middle aged man then started to walk across the car park.

I was suddenly shy. I didn't know what to say but I knew that I had to speak to him. I got up and walked towards him. Merlin stopped when he saw me and I felt my face getting red as his blue eyes looked into mine. His hands were in his pockets and for a long moment he just stood and looked at me. I wished I were prettier. I wished I was like other girls and could talk easily to boys. I wished I could speak better English.

'I wanted to know what was to happen to you,' I managed to say at last.

'You are not English,' he said and my heart sank. I was not pretty enough and a foreigner. He would be like many of the English boys who shout at the foreign students, telling them to go home.

'No. I am from Portugal,' I replied and turned to walk away.

'I thought you wanted to know what happened.' The words were said slowly and carefully and I thought how deep his voice was for a boy. I turned back. I couldn't reply; all I could do was nod.

We sat in the shade on the bench and I shared my lunch. In the space of an hour we learnt all about each other's lives. I told him about Sagres, my parents, my sister Ana and my uncle and aunt. Mine was an ordinary story, Merlin's sounded as though it had come from a story book I might have found in the library.

His mother had been a drug addict and had died when he was eight. His father was an alcoholic who spent all their money on drink and Merlin was left to look after his two sisters, Holly who was fourteen and Emma, thirteen. Emma was very unhappy and kept trying to run away. Merlin had tried to get help but for reasons I didn't understand he couldn't. He did know that if he got into trouble with the police and went to court, he would get help. He had picked a small shop to make certain he was seen and arrested. The court appearance had been what he had expected and he was due to go back to court in two weeks when a report on him and his family had been prepared.

The church clock had just struck one when he stood up and said he had to go. He was a head taller than me and although only seventeen, he looked and sounded so grown up. I wanted to say can we meet again, but he made me feel nervous, like a small child. He seemed so serious. In all the time we had been talking, he hadn't smiled. He must have been very worried but he was calm. His life was so very complicated and I wished I could help but what could I do? Perhaps I should give him my mobile number, but what if he said he didn't want it? I couldn't bear the thought of being disappointed.

In the end 'I hope everything goes well,' was all I said. He nodded and walked away across the churchyard without a backward glance. It was all I could do not to run after him.

For days afterwards, I was silent and unhappy and wished I had been brave enough to speak. All I could think about was Merlin's black hair and blue eyes; his nose, his mouth, his broad shoulders and strong hands. I imagined him in a black cloak riding on a white horse, imagined him rescuing me from danger. I tried to read or to think of other things but it was impossible.

It was Friday, almost two weeks later before I saw him again. Coming home from college I found him standing outside my uncle's shop. My heart beat faster and I fought the desire to rush up to him.

'I waited for you,' he said. He looked worried, nervous. 'Emma has disappeared again. I need to find her and wondered if you would help. She sometimes hides in toilets in the town…,' he hesitated, looked at me. 'I can't go into the women's toilets. Will you help look for her?'

It took me a moment to realise what he was asking.

'Yes, of course,' I said. 'We must go at once.'

Although I knew he was worried about his sister, I was happy. So very happy that he had asked me!

It took two hours but we found her, not in a toilet but in the local park. Emma was not at all like her brother. She was pale, blonde, thin and nervous. Only the eyes, bright blue, were the same. I suggested I bought us all burgers and we went to a café outside the park. While they ate I watched Merlin with his sister. He obviously loved her a lot and despite his anxiety was kind and calm with her.

'Why is your name Merlin?' I asked as we drank cola.

'My mother had stupid romantic ideas sometimes. She liked all those legends, especially the ones about Merlin. She told me once that Merlin wasn't the name of just one person. There were lots of Merlins. They were like witch doctors I suppose, the wise ones in a tribe. It's also the name of a bird, a hawk. I like my name!' he added defiantly. I could imagine that he must have been teased about his name many times.

I told him about my name, Matilde, and for the first time since I had met him he smiled. His smile was wonderful, his blue eyes crinkled up and his whole face changed. It was no longer the face of a man with worries but the face of a teenage boy.

'I like the idea of you going fearless into battle. I think the name suits you. You are fearless and thank you for helping to find Emma. But now I must take Emma home.'

He was going to disappear again. I felt my heart race and the happiness I had been feeling, faded immediately. I had to say something.

'It is Monday when you are to go to court again. Can I come and wait outside for you?'

'Oh, yes, Monday.'

'College will have finished, so I can be free for the whole day. I am going home to Portugal for the holidays on Friday but I would like to know what happens before I leave.'

He didn't reply, only nodded, then he and Emma were gone and I felt suddenly alone.

The weekend seemed to last forever but finally it was Monday and I sat on the same bench watching the entrance to the court. The morning passed slowly but eventually he came out. As he crossed the car park coming towards me, he was grinning.

'A year's probation,' he shouted.

We sat on the bench together. I thought that the result was terrible but he explained that it was good. For a whole year, the probation service would give him and his sisters help. Other social agencies would be involved too. There was a worry that their father's drinking or Emma's behaviour might get worse, but if things did, then they would intervene.

'I am sorry that I had to steal the bottle from your uncle, but it was the only way I could think of getting help.' Merlin stopped and looked at me with those piercing blue eyes and my heart beat so hard I thought he would hear it.

'I suppose he will always think of me as a thief?' Again, there was that defiant look.

'No, I have explained. My uncle knows how difficult things have been for you.'

Merlin stood up and held out his hand for me to shake. 'Thanks.' he said. 'Not just for helping me find Emma, but for...', he hesitated and looked embarrassed, '...you know, for waiting around. I appreciate it.'

He said it as though he didn't really mean it and I knew then that this time he would disappear and I wouldn't see him again.

I took his hand and felt a thrill run through my body at his touch. It was in that moment that I realised what my feelings for him meant. But this was it. He was saying goodbye.

I took my phone out of my pocket.

'Please. Let me give you my number. You never know. Maybe you will need help to find Emma again.' Anything to keep him with me for another minute or so.

He took his phone out of his trouser pocket and typed in my number. He smiled briefly at me then was gone, this time running across the churchyard as though glad to get away from me.

I had never felt so unhappy. It had been stupid of me to think he might ever be interested in me, a foreigner, nothing special. Just a girl from Portugal, in his country to learn his language.

I packed my suitcase on Thursday for the journey to Portugal and thought about the long summer at home. Suddenly I didn't want to go home. Even if Merlin didn't want to see me, if I stayed in England at least I was closer to him. But the ticket for the plane was already in my bag and I told myself that I was crazy. I had meant nothing to him. At home perhaps I would soon forget about an English boy with blue eyes and an unusual name.

My phone beeped. A message, probably from my aunt. I switched it on and retrieved the message.

'Don't get into any battles while you are away Matilde. Can I see you when you come back? Merlin,' and after his name xx.

— ಇಲ —

ACTIVITY 1 Predicting the story line

1.1 Read the following extracts and match each extract with one of the titles on the right. In pairs, discuss your choice of titles.

A. But if you will love me and let me be your companion and playmate, and let me sit beside you at the table, eat from your little golden plate, drink out of your little cup, and sleep in your little bed—if you promise me all that, I'll dive down and retrieve your golden ball.	**The Selfish Giant**
	The Frog King
B. "I will stay with you always," said the Swallow, and he slept at the Prince's feet.	**Merlin**
	The Happy Prince
C. "It was you," said the prince, "who saved my life when I lay dead on the beach," and he folded his blushing bride in his arms.	**The Little Mermaid**
	Romeo and Juliet
D. Thus with a kiss I die.	
E. Don't get into any battles while you are away, Matilde. Can I see you when you come back?	**The Canary Prince**

1.2 Work individually for a few minutes and think what this story is about. Look at the title only and put some more words, ideas, images or symbols in the box below. Compare your ideas and predictions about the story with a partner.

1.3 In pairs, choose ten of the words below that you think may appear in the story. Present your lists to the class and explain the reasons for your choice.

enchantment   kingdom
adventure   castle   dashing
magic   shining   protection
gallop   escape   vulnerable
threaten   haunt   bewitched
grin   supernatural   restore
fight   nod   wizard   rescue
dangers   knights   powers
court   police   armour

My list	My partner's list
1	1 ....
2	2 ....
3	3 ....
4	4 ....
5	5 ....
6	6 ....
7	7 ....
8	8 ....
9	9 ....
10	10 ....

ACTIVITY 2 Forming and describing first impressions

Listen to the whole story just once (your teacher can read it to you if you do not have the recording) and then write down all you can remember. Do not worry if you have not understood everything and if you cannot remember details. Read the story and compare your notes with the original.

The story as I remember it

ACTIVITY 3   Posting comments on a blog

Read the extract below and write a similar paragraph about your own reading experiences. Then post it to your Reading Class blog. Post comments on at least two entries submitted by other members of your class.

> I loved all the old stories of knights and princesses, dragons and pirates but the legend of Arthur and Guinevere was my favourite. I dreamt of the day when a dashing knight would come along and turn me into his princess. It might seem an impossible dream but sixteen is a time to think that anything is possible, even a knight in shining armour galloping into your life on a white horse.

My reading experiences

ACTIVITY 4   Acting out a court-room drama

You are going to act out Merlin's trial in groups. Before you begin, match the people on the left with the descriptions on the right and then compare your answers with the other members of your group. Select and prepare your roles, making sure that each member of the group understands their role. Add or delete roles depending on the size of your group. Finally, act out the scene in front of the class, who will play the members of the public. Will the members of the jury agree? Will they reach a verdict? Will the judge pass a sentence? There are many possibilities so be creative and do not be afraid to improvise.

Members of the public	Takes down notes of what is said in court
Barrister	Describe their side of the course of events; may be cross-examined to check the accuracy or credibility of their evidence
Public prosecutor	Appears before the court charged with an offence
Judge	Hear the evidence and decide if the defendant is innocent or guilty
Stenographer	People observing the proceedings in court
Defendant	Represents the defendant in court.
Witnesses	Tries to prove that someone accused of an offence is guilty
Members of the jury	Conducts the proceedings in court and decides how a guilty person is to be punished

Key roles for Merlin's trial:

Merlin – Matilde – Matilde's uncle – Matilde's aunt – Merlin's two sisters

ACTIVITY 5 Producing a haiku

In pairs, write a haiku, a three-line poem, to summarise the content of the story. The first line should have five words, the second seven words and the final line five words. When you finish, enter your poem for the Class Poem Competition. Put them on the classroom wall/board and read them all. Reflect on the poems and decide which you think is best. Follow the instructions of your teacher to hold a secret ballot in order to vote for the best poem.

To help you, here is an example of a three-line poem using the 5-7-5 pattern:

In Suffolk, Matilde learnt English.
Blue-eyed Merlin stole brandy and her heart
Good-bye, but please come back!

Now write another haiku on a subject of your own choice. It can be about anything you like, a person, an experience, an emotion. As always, be creative!

ACTIVITY 6   Discussing opinions found on an internet forum

Read the opinions below posted in answer to a question on a discussion forum.

Do fairy tales encourage damaging social and gender expectations?

CT says:
Promoting happily-ever-after endings in stories creates unreal expectations in children.
Do you agree? Yes No

GentleJanet says:
Children believe that everything will be fine because someone or something will change their life for them.
Do you agree? Yes No

Speedo says:
Female equality and emancipation are overemphasised in modern society.
Do you agree? Yes No

Kelley23 says:
Men have two roles: emotionless prince or hero.
Do you agree? Yes No

P3rf3ct_10 says:
Girls expect perfection. Boys know that they cannot ever achieve perfection.
Do you agree? Yes No

HonestJim says:
Being a traditional man is increasingly becoming very negative.
Do you agree? Yes No

Work in pairs and discuss each of the statements in turn. Draw lots to see whether you AGREE or DISAGREE with each statement. Provide arguments and examples to support the point of view you have drawn. After five minutes, go to the next statement and repeat the procedure. Then share your own opinions with the class.

Image credits

Page 11, 16, 19, 22, 24, 32,40, 43,47, 59, 63, 67, 69, 84, 90,92,96,99 Dreamstime, 26,37,70,89 Dreamstime & MC, 32 Clapboard MC, Girl with camera – public domain under CC 1.0 Universal, 52, 58 public domain, 65 and 76 "Korean.culture-PC.bang-01" by Hachimaki http://flickr.com/photos/robfahey/146145429/. Licensed under CC BY-SA 2.0 via Wikimedia Commons - http://commons.wikimedia.org/wiki/File:Korean.culture-PC.bang-01.jpg#/media/File:Korean.culture-PC.bang-01.jpg, 74 Depositphotos, 76 Imperial Hotel Castlemaine by freeaussiestock.com, licensed under CC 3.0 Unported http://freeaussiestock.com/free/Victoria/slides/hotel_castlemaine.htm, Boeing 747 at Glasgow Airport forNS4766 Copyright Thomas Nugent licensed under CC BY 2.0 http://www.geograph.org.uk/photo/579731, 80 Two Female Pet Rats released under GNU Free Documentation License and CC SA 3.0 Unported http://commons.wikimedia.org/wiki/File:Two_Female_Pet_Rats.JPG, 80 Two Girls On Phone CC0 Public Domain http://pixabay.com/de/afrika-m%C3%A4dchen-gespr%C3%A4ch-am-telefon-713336, Light at the end of the tunnel by Dusan Bicanski, Public domain via Wikimedia Commons http://commons.wikimedia.org/wiki/File: Light_on_door_at_the_end_of_tunnel.jpg, Two tails cat by Scorpius02 licensed under CC 3.0 Unported (CC BY 3.0) http:/scorpius02.deviantart.com/art/Two-tails-cat-153333106, Smoke Plume by William Warby CC BY 2.0 https://www.flickr.com/photos/wwarby/11775285796, Cloth Rags by Sherrie Thai, CC BY 2.0 https://www.flickr.com/photos/shaireproductions/7076823475, 83 Depositphotos, 84 http://en.wikipedia.org/wiki/Bill_Gold#/media/File: CasablancaPoster-Gold.jpg, "CasablancaPoster-Gold" by Bill Gold http://www.impawards.com/1942/casablanca.html Public Domain, Ambush Valley http://commons.wikimedia.org/wiki/File: Ambush_Valley_-_movie_poster.jpg, Public domain, http://commons.wikimedia.org/wiki/File: Wizard_of_oz_movie_poster.jpg, http://commons.wikimedia.org/wiki/Category: Sintel#/media/File: Sintel_poster.jpg Sintel: CC 3.0, Metropolis CC BY 2.0 https://www.flickr.com/photos/39453315@N04/3702272322/in/photostream/Les Miserables CC BY 2.0 https://www.flickr.com/photos/39453315@N04/3701278287/in/photostream/, 101 CC0 Public Domain: http://pixabay.com/de/formular-stift-dokument-schreiben-656262/, http://www.picgifs.com/clip-art/magic-tricks/clip-art-magic-tricks-291144-671175/, 104 Shakespeare blog By Cambodia4kids.org CC BY 2.0 https://www.flickr.com/photos/cambodia4kidsorg/267060150

Further ELT titles from LinguaBooks

Academic Presenting and Presentations
A preparation course for university students
By Peter Levrai and Averil Bolster

This practical training course is designed to help students cultivate academic presentation skills and deal with the variety of presentation tasks they may need to master during their studies. The material is suitable for a global audience and can be used in a wide range of academic contexts since the content not only helps learners develop their presentation skills in English but also considers wider topics relevant to English for Academic Purposes, such as principles of research and the risk of plagiarism. The accompanying online video presentations enable learners to immerse themselves still further in the material presented and witness first hand the impact of the techniques illustrated.

The European Journal of Applied Linguistics and TEFL
Edited by Andrzej Cirocki

The *European Journal of Applied Linguistics and TEFL* (EJALTEFL) is a refereed academic publication published twice yearly to disseminate information, knowledge and expertise in applied linguistics with a special focus on English language teaching. This provides a valuable source of reference for linguists, teacher trainers, materials developers and others in the field of EFL/ESL. Each issue offers key insights into current topics, broadening the reader's knowledge and promoting professional development.

Controversies in ELT
What you always wanted to know about teaching English but were afraid to ask
By Maurice Claypole

In this collection of controversial essays on English language teaching, which includes chapters on **The Death of the Communicative Approach, Teaching the Language of Sex, Non-native User Teachers** and **Parapsychology in ELT,** the author seeks to both inform and entertain.

'This book provides a refreshing look at old concepts, opens our eyes to new perspectives and encourages teachers to venture along new paths.'
- Elke Schulth

Teaching EFL Online
An e-moderator's report
By Andrew R. Webster

This study explores the role played by the e-moderator in creating and teaching an online course in English as a Foreign Language. It details relevant theories of online learning and shows how they are represented through various models, creating a framework to assist the e-moderation process.

EFL Communication Strategies in Second Life
An exploratory study
By Susan Gowans

This book reports the findings of an exploratory case study examining the communication strategies used between a small group of adult EFL learners and their teacher during meaning-focused conversation tasks in the virtual 3D world of Second Life. Discourse analysis of the session transcript offers insights into areas of language such as power relations, politeness and risk taking strategies.

The Fractal Approach to Teaching English as a Foreign Language
Dynamism and Change in ELT
By Maurice Claypole

The fractal approach envisages a new paradigm of language based on forms found in nature and indicates a goal-oriented method of developing teaching materials incorporating a holistic view of language acquisition.

'With this approach, Claypole steps away from ELT convention and offers a perspective from a very different world… His contribution to the field is definitely worth reading.'
- Evan Frendo

Artificial Intelligence in Autonomous Language Learning
An Expert System Approach to Computer Assisted EFL Self Study
By Maurice Claypole

Despite major advances in computer hardware generally and in software development techniques in areas such as engineering troubleshooting and gaming, computer assisted foreign language learning applications have not kept pace with the general trend. This is as true today as it was when the content of this book was first set out and in a sense we are still waiting for the envisaged breakthrough which will harness the power of artificial intelligence and object-oriented software development in order to create truly effective software solutions specifically designed for the independent language learner.

The second edition of this book presents a snapshot in time outlining the scope of software solutions available for autonomous language learning at an early stage of their development and then goes on to examine the interface between the technology of expert systems and the characteristics of natural language processing.

www.linguabooks.com